Teaching Language-Disordered Children

Teaching Language-Disordered Children

A Structured Curriculum

Ella Hutt

ICAA Curriculum Development and Resource Unit,
John Horniman School

Edward Arnold

© Ella Hutt 1986

First published in Great Britain 1986 by
Edward Arnold (Publishers) Ltd, 41 Bedford Square, London WC1B 3DQ

Edward Arnold (Australia) Pty Ltd, 80 Waverley Road, Caulfield East,
Victoria 3145, Australia

Edward Arnold, 3 East Read Street, Baltimore, Maryland 21202, USA

British Library Cataloguing in Publication Data

Hutt, Ella
 Teaching language-disordered children.
 1. Children —— Language 2. Communicative disorders in children 3. Language
 arts— Remedial teaching
 I. Title
 371.9'043 LC4704
 ISBN 0-7131-6459-X

Text set in 10/11 pt English Times
by Colset Pte Ltd, Singapore
Printed and bound in Great Britain by
Thomson Litho Ltd, East Kilbride, Scotland

Contents

Acknowledgements

I would like to express my gratitude to Muriel Gillies, head teacher of John Horniman School, and other teachers and speech therapists, Sylvia Cowper, Joy Davis, Christine Houghton, Mary Jennings, Sally Jones, Judy Marsden and John Parrott, for their help and encouragement in so many ways;

Molly Palmer, former head teacher of the school, who faithfully helped to edit each chapter as soon as it was written, and saved me by her memory, advice and commonsense from omissions, errors and circumlocutions;

Margaret Campkin, who generously allowed me to use long quotations from and paraphrases of the texts she has written on Musicolour and educational drama;

Jill Hutchinson, Sally Jones and Monica Walter, who checked the chapters on art and craft, LARSP and Margaret Morris Movement respectively;

Pauline Garthwaite and Ronald Senator, for allowing me to quote from their personal communications;

Dilys Hodges, for untiringly typing and re-typing the manuscript; and Joy Bellamy, who cheerfully joined in the time-consuming tasks at the final stages of its presentation;

Christopher Donlan, deputy head teacher of John Horniman School, who offered to be the reader of the entire typescript;

Martin Booker, who took all the photographs;

Messrs Churchill Livingstone for permission to quote from Gordon and McKinlay's book.

the parents of the two boys whose reports comprise the Appendix, for permission given on behalf of their sons, to include them; and the speech therapists who wrote the pre-entry speech therapy reports on one of the boys, and a girl;

the 333 children who have been pupils at the school, for all they have taught us;

the committee of the ICAA Curriculum Development and Resource Unit, especially Pauline Griffiths, who encourages and advises whenever necessary;

and my publishers, Edward Arnold, for their editorial advice and encouragement.

Ella Hutt
November 1985

1. Introduction

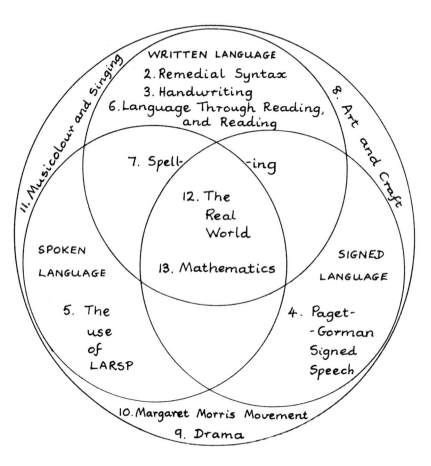

1 Introducing the children and the curriculum

Two children are talking to a teacher about a picture. They are asked, 'What's Mummy doing?' Ted says, 'She's cleaning up.' 'No', says Andrew, 'she's cleaning down.' But Ted repeats, 'Cleaning up', and the teacher supports him. 'Yes, cleaning up, Andrew.' But Andrew has the last word, 'No. Cleaning down, in the cellar. Cleaning up, in the bedroom.' Most people have experienced this kind of confusion in the use of phrasal verbs by children of two or three years of age. But Andrew is an intelligent seven-year-old.

Susan and Nicky are talking to each other. 'Is Christmas at Easter?' enquires Nicky, who wonders if the imminent Easter holiday will contain the delights of the previous Christmas break. But Susan's time sense is slightly more advanced. 'No, silly. It's in November.' By this time, Nicky has forgotten his original question, and corrects Susan, 'Not November. Decover.' She and Nicky have average intelligence and are eight years old.

Edward is six. A speech therapist is asking what he plans to do at the weekend. (His poor phonology has not been transcribed.)

Therapist:	What are you doing tomorrow?
Edward:	Home in car, and sweets.
Th:	What will you do at home?
E:	Play Kim.
Th:	Who's Kim?
E:	New dog.
Th:	Where does Kim sleep at night?
E:	Sleeping. My room.
Th:	Where?
E:	On bed.

Charles is listening to a conversation between two adults. Charles is also six.

Adult A:	Who was that at the front door?
Adult B:	Mr X locked himself out.

Charles is showing more concern than the occasion demands. 'Did he really?' he asks. Five minutes later he is still worried. 'Did Mr X really knock himself out?'

All these errors are typical results of severe disorders of language in young school-age children with average or above average intelligence. There has recently been a sharp increase in the identification of such disorders. Those that are considered not to be the result of low intelligence, or hearing loss, or autism, or emotional disorder, are described as 'specific' language disorders. They occur in all strata of society, and vary in degree.

The types of language disorder

They are many, but most can be recognized among five main categories;

- relating to the system used by each child to vocalize the *sounds* he thinks he is perceiving (phonological disorder); this is remediated mainly by speech therapists, who also advise teachers and others on attitudes and approaches to this aspect of each child's difficulty;
- relating to the system used by each child to *sequence the words* he tries to say (syntactic disorder);
- relating, in this context, to the *word-endings* which modify the meanings of the words to which they are joined (morphological disorder);

(grammatical disorder)

- relating to the *meaning* of words, sentences, etc. (semantic disorder);
- relating to the *use* of language (pragmatic disorder). This book provides no specific guidelines to the remediation of this kind of difficulty.

In some children more than one disorder is discernible. It is often difficult to estimate from which areas such misunderstandings and immaturity as those quoted above arise.

Two typical examples

The John Horniman School, opened in 1958, is a residential school for 24 of these children, between the ages of five and nine. About two-thirds of them are boys. About a third of the children have severe receptive disorders. Excerpts from a speech therapist's report of a girl aged 4 years 3 months, who subsequently entered the school, describe a typical example.

She presents as a bewildered child. Her expressive language comprises single words interspersed with jargon which occasionally has the intonation of normal speech. Her vocabulary consists of single names of objects, and a few verbs. She is able to copy isolated speech sounds, but not a sequence of sounds. She makes attempts to communicate by gesture, noise and facial expressions, but the level of her communication is very limited. Spoken language means very little to her. Her response to any sound is inconsistent; for instance, she will respond to her name one day and not another. She is able to sort objects according to colour, shape and size, if shown visually. She is quick to grasp concepts. She likes things to be lined up and laid out in an exact visual pattern, and can be quite persistent and obsessional about this. It would seem that she has an auditory imperception which makes following any verbal instruction very difficult, and learning expressive language a great problem.

All children like this who have such great difficulty in the comprehension of verbal language have a comparable difficulty in its production. They have received little, and therefore have limited means of expressing even the little they have understood.

Other children, however, whose verbal comprehension skill is only minimally impaired, share the expressive difficulty. The other two-thirds of the children are in this group. Edward's speech therapist wrote about him when he was 4½ years old:

Edward's speech therapy began when he was 3½ years old. It was felt that he would benefit from a small language group. After a few months he was given more concentrated individual therapy, but he reacted badly to this and refused to cooperate altogether, showing anger and temper tantrums on many occasions. He now attends a weekly pre-school language group. He appears happy, and is able to understand and participate successfully in many exercises.

However he still finds it very difficult to tolerate his frustration at his own expressive difficulty, and is often disruptive, showing aggression to the other children and to the therapists. If, when he refuses to cooperate, he is ignored, he eventually returns to the group.

He is within the normal range of intelligence. He appears to comprehend everything, and has no difficulty in following commands.

Expression is his main area of difficulty. His expressive speech consists mainly of single unclear words, accompanied by much gesture, miming and grunting. He is obviously keen to communicate and uses every means available to him, but is unable to cope with his frustration and therefore often gives up in a fit of anger.

The words he uses bear very little resemblance to the correct form, and the sounds he is able to produce are limited. He is unable and unwilling to make a concentrated effort to try to imitate words clearly; and his auditory memory is short. He finds it difficult to retain and reproduce more than one sound at a time. He is able to copy individual sounds, and often uses one sound to indicate a whole word or phrase.

Most of his communication is effected by the gestures he has been forced to invent for himself.

Each of these two children has an average non-verbal IQ, normal hearing, no primary emotional disorder, and a strong desire to communicate. Typically, the expressive spoken language of this school's population, if present at all, comprises strings of *open-class words** and a few prepositions. Pronouns are usually substituted for each other. There is no implicit tense-distinction. Most noun determiners and parts of the verb 'to be' are omitted. Negatives and conjunctions are rare.

Teaching the children

When children of this kind were admitted to the first two residential special schools for them in England, Moor House School Oxted, Surrey in 1946, and John Horniman School, Worthing, Sussex in 1958, their teachers searched in vain for any information describing methods of educating them. The current thinking at that time was that all remediation was given by speech therapists, in the speech therapy clinic which was separate from the school. Teachers were there to give the children normal education, which may have had to be slightly modified; and the school kept the children until their speech had reached an acceptable standard for being admitted to a local school. The speech therapists had become aware of some of the children's language needs, and begun to experiment with new remediation techniques. But as there were almost no relevant objective tests, it was difficult to plan treatment in detail. And the best available ideas for teachers came from North American books describing work with a much broader population of children, those with many kinds of learning disorders.

Although current speech therapy training includes more advanced methods of detailed analysis, providing basic information for individual treatment, and also a number of remedial techniques, there is still only a limited amount of parallel information for teachers. Since 1979 many have been appointed to new language units, attached to at least 200 primary schools. The children in some of these units are integrated into the parent school. The concept of integration is interpreted differently according to local needs and resources: consequently the teacher–child ratio differs between units. More teachers are asking for more help.

This book, based on a quarter of a century's experience in teaching children with severe specific language disorders, is designed as a step towards meeting this need, by describing the content and method used in some areas of one school's curriculum. In 1958 the teachers at John Horniman School were in a comparable situation when we were each confronted with a class of children with problems in the understanding

*See Glossary for italicized terms.

and use of language. Our immediate response was to think at a very basic level of tasks with which to occupy them. This was followed by attempts to teach them, with varying degrees of success. Obvious grammatical errors were among those we chose to put right, for example, past tense forms. This resulted in a number of ungeneralized learned usages which had no relation at all to what is now known about the normal development of spoken language. It was not until we asked ourselves questions about the nature of these children's learning difficulties, and made some attempt to put ourselves in their place, that we were able to devise teaching methods which were more suitable than the discovery methods which were commonly accepted at that time. Gradually an appropriate curriculum began to emerge. The methods for teaching the several aspects of language were an intrinsic part of the curriculum itself. It gradually became apparent that both the content of the curriculum and the methods of presenting it must be highly structured. The necessity for this is emphasized in an extract from a talk given by a former head teacher of the school.

One of the main problems for teachers confronted by these complex and difficult children is to know where to start. Assessment will usually reveal that the language disordered child has at his disposal odd items of unrelated information and a few rote skills, some of which can look and sound quite impressive, but what he has in fact acquired are those skills which come most easily, are superficial, and meaningless in terms of real cognitive development. They paper over large chasms of ignorance and confusion, and there is no depth of understanding. The only effective option is figuratively to strip the learning situation right down and find out by careful observation and standardized tests exactly where the child is developmentally. On the basis of this, a structured programme must be designed in order to remediate the deficiencies, and situations contrived conducive to learning taking place. Let no teacher assume that a normal classroom environment and good 'normal' teaching will fill the gaps. They will not. In fact, quite the opposite: and educational philosophy allowing freedom of choice is not only ineffective but can be positively harmful to the language disordered child, as the inflow of stimuli from an enriched environment only serves to confuse and distract him, and he is unable to distinguish the relevant from the irrelevant. This kind of freedom of choice is equally potentially damaging owing to his lack of integration, discrimination and awareness, and he becomes more and more insecure and unable to concentrate on a single issue.

Probably what teachers find most difficult to accept in the dysphasic child is his abnormal, not merely low, level of reasoning and representational ability. Even experience of other types of handicapped children is little or no preparation for the devastating effect of his rigidity and literal-mindedness, his inability to see relationships and classify, to learn by experience and adjust to new situations, to abstract principles and apply them, and to understand global concepts. Many handicapped children pick up a good deal of their education by a kind of osmosis; this is not the case with the language disordered child. He needs carefully planned *teaching* at the right level, with constant checking and revision to ensure that he first understands and then retains what he has learnt, and the fact that his auditory memory is usually deficient makes this more than normally difficult. He is a slow learner and a quick forgetter. He appears to lack most of the essentials for normal mental functioning, even though his non-verbal potential may be average.

Normal language acquisition begins in the spoken medium. But where this is disordered, the learning process is inverted. The use of auditory perception must be bypassed, and optimum use must be made of the skills of visual perception. So manual signs and written words often precede spoken words. Because the disorder hinders the testing of reading ability by speech, the problem must be overcome by a method in which production skills precede comprehension. So a child learns to associate single written words with meaning, and to sequence these, before he learns to decode printed sentences. Thus, not only do reading and writing precede speech, but also writing precedes reading. In practice, the use of signs, written words and spoken words are so interrelated that in most of the less handicapped children this precedence is imperceptible.

The John Horniman curriculum

The curriculum can be described as a system of systems. Some have been devised in response to individual needs, and later used to help children with different needs. This is the reason why each aspect is described in broad terms. Each one is so flexible that it can be freely modified and be applied as successfully. Some of the systems, such as Paget–Gorman Signed Speech, Margaret Morris Movement and Musicolour have been adopted and adapted. But the unifying factor is the vocabulary employed in the early stages of using each of the systems.

The core vocabulary for core concepts

The core vocabulary is based on three frequency lists, in studies which were carried out in different situations, but with children of six years old. The Burroughs list (1957) is the earliest one used. Spontaneous spoken vocabulary used in a free classroom situation, a home-corner, was counted. In their (1964) book, *Words your children use*, Edwards and Gibbon recorded the written vocabulary most frequently used in classroom assignments. The subjects of both these studies were British. Those in the third study, *The language of children: a key to literacy*, were Australian. Hart, Walker and Gray (1977) studied the development of spoken vocabulary during the first six years of the lives of their subjects.

From these three studies were taken those words common to at least two of them, and usually to all three. A core list of between 700 and 800 words was produced. This is used as the basis for work in every aspect of the curriculum. But given a child with almost no vocabulary, it is not desirable, nor even possible, to start with the same words in every area of the curriculum. In vain does anyone look for words which are as easy to say as they are to write, or sign, or read, or spell: they do not exist. Imagine the difference between a bunch of flowers in the hand and a similar bunch in a V-shaped vase. The bottoms of the stalks of the first bunch do not touch each other; those of the second bunch are so close that they may appear as one. The language disordered curriculum must resemble the first bunch. Vocabulary is sorted in different ways, based not only on children's needs, but also on ease of recognition or production. Short words may be easier to spell, but longer ones are easier to recognize: labials are simpler to lip-read, but gutturals are easier to say: although it would appear more logical to teach phonic associations by starting with short vowels, experience proves that long vowels written with digraphs are more easily distinguished from each other. These are just some of the paradoxes inherent in the construction of an integrated curriculum. Other expectations are also proved incorrect. For example, colour is used in many different contexts, to aid discrimination between word classes, between sounds, between numbers, and between the duration or the pitch of musical notes: but the children do not get confused between these different uses. Showing distinctions which are greater than binary, colour is indispensable to them, and their intelligence overcomes the potential additional confusion.

The common core-vocabulary thus unites the different aspects of the curriculum. No remediator extends her pupils' vocabulary until they are ready for such an extension. At that stage it is no longer necessary to restrict the number of words, presented in whatever medium. The stalks of the flowers are now in the vase. The several aspects of language are being integrated, by different children at different levels. Usually the points of integration are not noticeable immediately, but only after they have become an established part of the child's spontaneous expressive language.

The common vocabulary is only one element of the structure implicit in the content and presentation of the curriculum. It is always present, like the letters in a stick of seaside rock. It is divided conceptually into four main meaning-types: people and things, represented by nouns and adjectives; actions, by main verbs; positions, by prepositions, adverbs and prepositional particles; and all the other vocabulary items are clumped together because they are all as difficult as time-words, impossible to define in terms of overlapping word-classes, and constitute the most important group of words to learn.

The concepts which words represent are one of the three planes of a

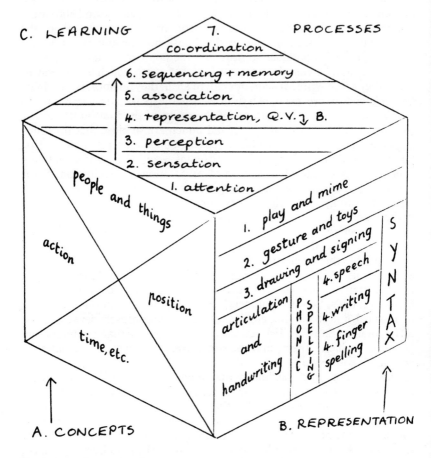

Figure 1.1   Structure cube

'structure cube' which models the framework of the curriculum as seen by a remediator. The other two dimensions are those of the stages of representation, and the children's learning processes.

Stages of representation
Not until a child uses representation in play can he be expected to realize that manual signs and words, written and spoken, have a comparable representational value. Not till he can pretend to be someone else or something else, and recognize that many toys are miniature versions of items in the real world around him, can he be introduced to the

arbitrariness of manual and verbal symbols. The obvious link between pretence or toys, and words, is drawing. Some children with severe disorders of language use this spontaneously as an effective means of communication. Its use should be encouraged.

Manual signs can be introduced fractionally earlier than words. Some of them are ideographic: the meaning of these is quickly apparent to anyone who has never experienced a signing environment; and they serve as a useful transition to more arbitrary manual signs and other symbol systems. Manual signs can be strung together to form phrases and sentences. Then whole words do the same. And it is on known lexical signs that word-ending signs can be seen as modifying agents. They are seen here first as wholes and later are transposed into written letters and into sound-groups, which can be added to known words, in both written and spoken media. Details about Paget–Gorman Signed Speech, the most suitable manual sign system in the context of language disorder, are given in Chapter 4.

At the same time the handwriting of single letters is learned. And spoken sounds are discriminated from each other, usually at the beginnings and ends of words. The phonic associations between sounds and letters are learned gradually. So whole words are being approached from another angle.

Primary associations are made between meaning and symbols: separately with manual signs, with written words, and with spoken words. Teachers must be aware of the danger of trying to teach the meaning of one symbol via another symbol. It is theoretically possible for a child's response to one symbol to be another symbol, neither of which has been associated with its meaning. Similarly it is necessary to check the comprehension of symbols in as many ways as possible: that is, not only with another arbitrary symbol, but also with drawing or small toy representation, or some kind of mime.

When syntactic sequences have been learned via manual signs, they are translated into words. When these can be strung together acceptably, then they are extended into longer word-strings, making paragraphs, letters and stories.

Learning processes
The third dimension of the structure cube comprises the main learning processes. With any kind of learning difficulty, the ability to pay attention visually, auditorily and intellectually is fundamental. No teacher can teach efficiently or the child learn if he is not looking, listening or thinking to the best of his ability. He may have only a limited control over his inability to concentrate, and the over-activity and distractability associated with it. However he is trainable, and this kind of training is already built into a programme structured in short steps, with clearly defined goals, which ensures early success, often a new experience to him, and consequent good motivation. But for some children it may be necessary to use a specific

attention training programme, such as that described in *Helping language development* (Cooper, Moodley and Reynell (1978)).

Some children need specific perceptual training. A few have such limited perception within their own bodies they do not feel the pain of a broken arm, nor recognize the unfamiliar and unpleasant taste of milk that is bitter as well as sour. They have fewer food preferences and dislikes than normal children, which probably indicates poor taste perception. Their auditory skills are far below the average of normal learners of the same age.

Associations of all kinds must be carefully taught: the relationships between people and people, things and things, people and things, people and actions, people and things in places and in time, their representation by gestures, manual signs, and spoken and written words, and the relationships between these types of symbols and between the symbols in each group. Teaching correct associations is probably the most accurate way of describing the task of a teacher of language disordered children. They must first be clearly understood by the teacher, and then presented to the children so well that there is no chance of misunderstanding.

Reading difficulties of all kinds are encountered. All but a few of the children learn this skill more slowly than their peers, for one or more reasons: from their problems of associating written and spoken symbols with each other, whether whole words or phonic associations; to their inability to understand the material once it has been decoded.

Although some theorists dispute the existence of sequencing as a separate skill, some language disordered children have great difficulties with it. This is apparent not only in written errors, typical of dyslexic children, but also in the conceptual sequencing of two or more drawings into a meaningful series. It is hard to separate this from difficulties in orientation, and from the reversals of cutlery when laying the table. It is probably that, for these children, binary distinctions are even more difficult than sequencing tasks.

Memory, both short-term and long-term, is also abnormal. Language disordered children have to make greater than the average effort to remember on a Monday morning what they did at the weekend. They find it hard to complete a task with several parts, and have to be constantly reminded to carry out routine tasks. But, once these have become firmly established, it is difficult to change the routine.

Coordination presents still further problems, in all its aspects; within the physical body; between thoughts and actions; with simple tools; and of all combinations of these.

It is against this background of learning processes that the teacher must think of new teaching methods, of adapting old ones, and of applying additional suggestions to what already proves successful. Although it is difficult to put oneself in the place of any language disordered child, any attempt to do so surely improves her understanding of his struggle to learn. She must teach him not only what to learn, but also how to do it. It is an advantage to him if she herself experiences a genuine minimal handicap, which some teachers claim to do.

The development of the curriculum

Handwriting and spelling were the first parts of the curriculum to be structured. Then 'Remedial Syntax' provided a framework for the teaching of written grammar. Words are written for each child on small slips of paper and stored in a personal folder. The words are colour-coded according to word class. Sentences are constructed according to colour patterns.

Paget–Gorman Signed Speech is a manual sign system which fulfils all the criteria required in any such system for use with children with specifically syntactic language disorders. Its main use in this context is as an aid to learning grammar. Every word is represented by a sign. So is every grammatical word-ending, and there are separate signs for all *closed-class words*. This results in potentially precise communication. Still more uses for the system continue to be found. A child with only a severe speech difficulty needs to sign only those words he cannot say well enough to be understood. Adults sign to children as stimuli to word-production: this is quicker than searching for pictures. Some children find that signing while reading helps them to read more meaningfully. The PGSS also shares the advantages of all manual sign systems, including that of gaining and holding the attention of distractable children.

The careful grammatical analysis of each child's expressive language, however minimal, is essential to the planning of detailed objectives. The Language Assessment and Remediation Screening Procedure (LARSP) is an ideal tool for this. Attainments, omissions and errors are categorized within several broad stages. At the same time utterances are scored at three basic levels: clause level, phrase level, and word ending level. The result is a simple grid to be used as a framework for thinking, by speech therapist and teacher remediators. Further, the desired goals of the combination of clause-level and phrase-level skills become immediately apparent.

A logical extension to written and spoken grammatical programmes, both aided by the manual sign system, was the addition of a printed aid to language-learning, that is, a set of books and other reading material. 'Language Through Reading' is in three parts, comprising more than 100 sets of items, some in the form of interrelating pictures and printed cards, and some booklets. They also provide a bonus: they are not only a language scheme, but also teach the children to read. They are designed for maximum flexibility, so can be used according to individual requirements.

A considerable amount of thought has been given to the maths curriculum, over many years, by many teachers in the school. A temptation to omit it altogether, on account of the web of problems it produced, was gradually overcome. And essential concepts have been distilled.

It is preferable that the suggestions made in this book should be judged only with reference to children with language disorders that are specific, for whom these methods have been devised, and with whom they have proved successful. Some of them have also been used by teachers whose pupils' language problems arise from handicaps which are more easily defined, such as low intelligence or impaired hearing. Those teachers have modified the methods to suit their own particular groups. Manual signs may be bigger, words fewer, expectations lower, but achievement is still perceptible. And speech therapists working in cooperation with teachers may find some classroom ideas which can be adapted for use with individual children or small groups.

This book aims to present one main system for many, but not all, areas of the curriculum. Music, drama, art and movement are included, both in the school and here. Physical education and religious education are both taught. Different kinds of structure have been attempted for Physical Education but so far no specific one has been chosen. Ideas for content and methods for Religious Education are described elsewhere, for those teachers who agree about its prime importance in this situation as much as in any other school. Fringe activities within each area also exist within each classroom, but to attempt to describe them all would be confusing and unproductive. The structured framework of content and method is described, and, where appropriate, base-lines are given. Each child starts at whatever level he has reached by the time he enters the school. One of the aims of his teachers is to level out his skills, so that his learning can be proceed more normally. This may result in concentrating more on a few aspects than on others, especially in the initial stages. Suggestions for teaching materials are made. Some have been published. (See the section at the end of the References.) Others can be collected or made by the teacher when they become necessary.

But writing a book about a curriculum can be compared to writing a report about a child. It shows where the gaps are. They remain to be filled.

NOTES
1 A handbook of any kind risks becoming out-of-date before it is published, or even before the writing is completed. Although the curriculum described here is in current use, it is unlikely that every teacher in the school would subscribe to every detail. A school without modifications, expansions and additions would be dead. This one is very much alive!
2 It was necessary to allocate gender for the purposes of generalization. Because two out of every three language disordered children are boys, all the references are to male children. It seemed obvious that, conversely, female pronouns should be used for all teachers.

2 Language through writing: Remedial Syntax

Imagine a six-year-old boy who, despite his average non-verbal intelligence, has not acquired spoken language in the normal way. He has spent at least a year in a class of 30 to 40 children, bewildered by the activity surrounding him. His method of coping with this situation varies, depending on his own personality and on the amount of information his parents and teachers have gleaned about his handicapping condition, and also on the way in which they have used this knowledge. It is not likely that his teacher will have had the time to investigate appropriate means of teaching him the basic skills which the rest of the class are acquiring in the usual untroubled way.

Now he is the newest member of a much smaller class in a special school. He soon finds that his previous failure is not being repeated. He is being taught with simple materials that he can understand. His teacher is satisfied when he achieves the tasks she has prepared for him. One of the teaching methods she uses is 'Remedial Syntax'.

In his infants' school, he has been presented with a number of words, most of them meaningless to him. He has occasionally managed to match a few of these words with detailed coloured pictures, but his teacher has not been pleased when he could not match the same pictures and words the next day. Most of the words were written or printed on white paper. Or, on the blackboard, they were written in white chalk. All these words looked the same to him. Now the words are written on coloured cards or with coloured chalk on the blackboard. Now he can see more differences than before. He is given his own word cards and a folder of his own to keep them in. Every day he takes out some of the words and puts them side by side. He copies them into an exercise book. When his teacher is satisfied with his work she gives him some more words. Some of the other children have a folder full of words. Perhaps his will get full too.

A sequence of grammatical structures

Remedial Syntax is a sequence of grammatical structures. As in the *Colour Pattern Scheme* (John Lea, 1970) different colours are assigned to different word-classes. The technique for its use is that of the folder-method of *Breakthrough to Literacy*. Sequence, colours and folders together result in an effective way of providing a child whose understanding and/or use of spoken language is non-existent or minimal, with a visual aid to learning the grammatical aspect of language, and the early stages of writing and reading.

Most children learn first to speak, then to decode print into meaning, and to encode speech into writing. *These* children learn through the Remedial Syntax scheme to read single words, and with them to compose simple sentences, which they immediately copy. Not until then are they expected to read, for meaning, comparable sentences written by someone else. They are learning language through writing and reading.

The colours used in Remedial Syntax are:

- yellow for verbs
- orange for nouns
- white for *noun-determiners*
- pink for pronouns and proper nouns
- green for adjectives
- blue for prepositions
- brown for adverbs
- red for 'not'
- purple for conjunctions

The strength of the folder is its word-slips, which can be sequenced, substituted and rearranged. Young children need to be able to handle words and experiment with the word-sequences of new structures. They know it is possible to make incorrect sequences, and there derive greater satisfaction from producing acceptable ones.

The first stages

It is important that the first few words a child learns match real experience. This is why the most common human nouns have been chosen, and easily demonstrable verbs: *boy, girl, man, woman* and, for example, *jumping, standing, walking* and *sleeping*. All the people are available in a school setting, and all these actions can be performed or mimed within a classroom. Sixteen permutations are more than enough in the early stages. The people have orange labels pinned on to them, 'man', 'woman', 'boy', or 'girl'. Before each one jumps, stands, walks, or 'sleeps', he is given a yellow verb-label 'jumping', 'standing', 'walking', or 'sleeping'. The actions are repeated, in slow succession, by each person in turn. The sentence-matrix remains on the blackboard, that is, 'The – is – ing'; and the human nouns and/or the verbs are altered in preparation for the succeeding action, or as a description of the preceding one. A few children are distracted by the length of verbs, and may need to be presented with the verb-root alone.

The child begins to make sense of the environment nearest him. He finds it easy to select the correct word-slips which match the bigger flash cards. Any child who is not yet ready for this can be given the flash-cards instead, perhaps with the smaller identical word written in the corner, which he learns to read subliminally.

Person–action pairs are repeated, and, while the boy is running, every other child selects the two words 'boy' and 'running'. He does not yet write them down. Before this happens he must be introduced to two more cards, a white 'the', and a short yellow 'is'. And, in preparation for this he learns to play a simple sequencing game, with blank cards, about the same size as normal playing-cards; a quarter of them are white, a quarter are orange, and the remaining half are yellow. The rules of the game can be made up while it is being played. Turns are taken, and the aim is to cover the surface of the table with identical colour patterns: white–orange–yellow–yellow. No other sequence is accepted, and incorrect ones can be penalized. The game is learnt quickly, enjoyed, and its lesson easily applied. Then a white 'the', an orange human noun, a yellow 'is' and a yellow main verb are taken by the teacher from each child's folder and scattered on his desk. He must arrange them in the order he has just learnt. Now the working routine has been established. Someone performs an action, all the children select the right words from their folders, arrange them on the table, or on a wooden rod or a plastic rack. Each copies his sentence into his exercise book. The teacher may have provided lines of the appropriate colour and length, onto which each child can copy his words. This is helpful, but not always necessary for all children. Children are encouraged to illustrate each sentence quickly, and to read and sign it simultaneously.

Plate 2.1   The sentence arranged on the rod and copied into the book is being signed.

Soon real actions can be dispensed with, and replaced with quick drawings such as pin-men as stimuli. The simpler the drawing, the more versatile stimulus it is. As soon as practicable, children are taught that the white–orange pair of cards can be removed, and the space filled with a specific name, written on a pink card. Thus real experience is re-introduced.

The same simple sentence-pattern is practised, with more nouns, proper names, and verbs. Open-class vocabulary is increased within a controlled list, according to the needs of each individual child and/or to express new ideas as they are introduced by the teacher. She gradually introduces new structures, such as 'the boy is little', 'the house is big', and 'the boy is eating the cake', 'the woman is drinking the tea'. She distributes new closed-class words when they are needed as part of a new structure that is being taught, for example: prepositions; *are, am, was, were*; and pronouns. They all have a specific place in the suggested scheme. Some words, such as 'they' and 'not' can be taught at any time after a specific place in the scheme, usually as each child expresses a need for them.

Most young language disordered children have had little or no experience of being questioned. It is vital that, from the child's first experience of this grammatical scheme, he is taught to associate appropriate question-words with each structure. When the first two questions are learned, the child must be encouraged to understand the difference between them. This is very hard for him. When he is asked, 'Who [is — ing]?' he must reply with a human noun. When he is asked, 'What [is X] doing?' he must use a yellow word. To facilitate learning, written question words are presented in the same colour as the expected answer. So 'Who?' is orange or pink, and 'What. . . . doing?' is yellow. Similarly, 'Where?' is blue, and so is 'When?' in the initial stages. (Both can be brown if an adverbial answer is required.) 'Whose?' is white, as it assumes the answer ' — 's', and the ' — 's' substitutes for a determiner. 'What colour?' and 'How many?' are both green, requiring adjectival answers. In the early stages, when questions are asked, phrase-answers are demanded, not complete sentences. There is no other way in which a teacher can check whether the difference between two questions is properly understood.

Wherever possible, it is important that each new structure is compared with the original 'the boy is running' question, or with another as early as possible in the scheme, for example, – '. . . John's cake' with '. . . the cake'.

As a child makes progress he needs fewer clues. He soon learns to copy words in the accepted order without the provision of coloured lines. He learns to leave on his rod the words which are included in all of his current sentences, such as 'the' and 'is'. When he is sure of attributing the correct meaning to all the words in each sentence, he no longer needs to illustrate them all. When the same words have been copied many times, they become part of his mental store, so he no longer needs to lay them on his rod. He learns to write sentences about events in the past and the future. He comes to recognize the function of each different structure, and can use different ones in the same piece of work. The time comes when he does not need colour coding for all new words. He understands the noun-ness of nouns, and the verb-ness of verbs. His word store outgrows his folder so he begins to use an alphabetical word-book, like a dictionary. It includes extra pages for *ch* – , *sh* – , *th* – and *wh* – words. He is becoming self-sufficient and enjoys writing spontaneously. Remedial Syntax has done its work.

The selection of vocabulary

As a child progresses through the Remedial Syntax structures he is also being helped to say the words, as he decodes them into speech, with or without the aid of manual signs to match each word and each grammatical word-ending. The same 750-word vocabulary is used as a basis for all that is prepared for him in all three modalities. Its sources are being described here, as the reading and writing medium is the one which uses the core vocabulary the most faithfully. A corpus of words which are spoken, and the signs to match them, is more likely to include ideas beyond this central core. This is to be encouraged in most circumstances, but not at the expense of the exclusion of too many important *closed-class* words.

The original John Horniman vocabulary list, included as the second appendix in the Remedial Syntax book, was assembled at numerous staff meetings at which words were discussed one by one, and voted on or off the final list.

The second attempt to produce a more realistic vocabulary used two existing frequency lists of the spontaneous expressive vocabulary of normal six-year-old children. These were the 'spoken' list of Burroughs (1957) and the 'written' list from the study by Edwards and Gibbon (1964). The two lists were compared. Words which appeared with the highest frequency on both were listed as the kernel goal-vocabulary. Words which appeared at a similar frequency level in only one list were assigned to two further parallel lists, 'extra spoken' and 'extra written'. The first comprised mainly food and clothes, and the second mostly the type of word like 'grandma', 'present', 'fairy', 'woods' and 'holiday'. A similar process was repeated, and resulted in a second-level vocabulary list. But in practice, in most situations the total number of 800-odd words were all included when new teaching materials of any kind were being devised.

Then, a third source-list was discovered, the one gathered by members of Mount Gravatt College of Advanced Education in Brisbane, Australia. Each child's utterances throughout a complete day were recorded. They were analysed into words and word sequences.

The second John Horniman list was revised with the deletion of the least useful words, and the addition of some words from the Australian list. The 750 words are grouped according to word-classes, and are available in

Table 2.1: *Initial stages of Grammatical Sequence (John Horniman School, 1985)*

No.	LARSP Stage	LTR Part	Questions	Clause-level	Phrase-level	Word-level
1	2	One (52 Books)	who?		D(the)N(animate)	
2	3		what . . . doing?			V-ing
3	3				auxiliary verb: is	
4	$2\frac{1}{2}$	and		$\dfrac{S}{DN}$ +	$\dfrac{V}{aux + V\text{-}ing}$	
5	2	Two			D N (inanimate)	
6	3	Level One (12 Books)	what is [adj.]? what is [DN] like? what colour is [DN]?		adjective	
7	3				copula: is	
8	$3\frac{1}{2}$			$\dfrac{S}{DN}$ +	$\dfrac{V}{cop\text{:}is}$ + $\dfrac{C}{adj}$	
9	$3\frac{1}{2}$		what is [DN V]-ing?	$\dfrac{V}{aux\text{:}is + V\text{-}ing}$ + $\dfrac{O}{DN}$		
10	$3\frac{1}{2}$		what is [DN V]-ing? what is [DN] doing?	$\dfrac{S}{DN}$ + $\dfrac{V}{aux\text{:}is + V\text{-}ing}$ + $\dfrac{O}{DN}$		
11	3		where?		preposition	
12	3				prep DN	
13	$3\frac{1}{2}$		where is [DN]?	$\dfrac{S}{DN}$ + V + $\dfrac{A}{prep\ DN}$		
14	2				V part, e.g. (stand) up	

order of frequency and also in alphabetical order, as both formats are useful to remediators for different purposes. Verbs are also sub-classified according to their transitivity. Further lists, comprising the same words, have been prepared as suggested sequences for whole-word spelling and for teaching phonic associations.

The flexibility of the scheme

One of the reasons for working with a structured framework is, not that there is no deviation from it, but that there is a structure from which to deviate, for a variety of reasons, and that, when it is necessary to return to the framework, there is a framework to which to return. Although the basic technique, vocabulary, and initial activities are the same in every classroom, each teacher makes supplementary material as the need arises. Much of this can be stored and re-used when a similar need occurs with a different child. Some children learn from the minimum amount of material, but most need different reinforcements as they encounter specific difficulties. The need for a greater variety of pictures, work-cards and further stimuli for spontaneous writing increases as children progress through the scheme. Gradually descriptive writing is followed by narrative work. Accounts of visits and other events are written. And in a residential school, letter-writing provides additional motivation. Most language disordered children do not find imaginative writing easy. But as they grow older, their writing style continues to become less stilted and more natural. They become able to monitor their own work, and find great pleasure in producing a result which is satisfying both to themselves and to others.

3 Handwriting

Some children with severe language disorders are so poorly coordinated that, even at seven years old, their pencils fail to hit not only the line, but even the page! Although a normal child's handwriting practice usually needs less supervision from his teacher than written composition or reading, this cannot be said for this group. There are times when, for the sake of other subjects for which handwriting is an important skill, it is necessary to abandon some of them temporarily in order to work on legibility and ease of production. Language disordered children cannot be expected to concentrate on these and on the content at the same time.

Children who rely so heavily on printed and handwritten words for their initial language learning must as soon as possible learn to write well enough to read what they have written. Everything which they write they also read, in order to reinforce the language in which their thoughts have been expressed. A scheme which was among the earliest evolved, through sheer necessity, has proved successful with most of the children. Some of them progress through the scheme very quickly, while others need repeated practice in the formation and relative size of letters, which includes spacing, before their learning speed increases during the joining and fluency stages.

Five stages of teaching progression

Progression from little or no handwriting skill to useful fluent writing is in five stages. A preliminary activity necessary for most children is pattern-making. Materials for the three central stages are made available to each child for copying, and sometimes tracing. If further practice sheets are needed at the fluency stage, the teacher makes them for individual children. The necessary tools comprise blackboard and chalk, large soft pencils and large sheets or books made of newsprint or lining paper, slightly harder normal-sized pencils and exercise-books, some with no lines, some with wide lines (18 mm) and some with narrower lines (12 mm or 8 mm). Tracing books and some large sheets of tracing paper are useful; also coloured felt markers. Crayons are not so practical as most varieties limit fluency.

It is advisable to teach handwriting to all members of the class at the same time. Much that can be learned about handwriting is 'caught, not taught'. Children reinforce each other's efforts, and morale can be kept high. The best time-table slot is immediately after a physical activity, particularly any session such as Margaret Morris Movement, in which an arm-swinging exercise has been included. Even when this is possible, a transition needs to be made between gross and fine motor coordination, with any or all of the following movements.

The beginning of any lesson

1 Standing in a clear space, the children swing their arms forward and backward and then round and round in either direction. In order not to tire one arm too much, each can be used alternately, and sometimes swung together. One arm will be found to be used naturally for writing; then each child is encouraged to use this one more often.

2 Holding one elbow with the opposite hand, the children draw anti-clockwise circles in the air. The teacher draws a circle on the board to show what they must aim for; and also does it in front of the children but in reverse. Very few children mentally reverse what the teacher does. This ensures that they practise the circles in the right direction.

3 Holding one wrist with the opposite hand they draw smaller circles, still 'in the air'.

4 Kneeling they draw circles on the floor with their forefingers.

5 They draw circles with their forefingers on their desks.

6 Each child holding a pencil as if for writing, i.e. between the thumb and first two fingers, the first finger acting as 'guide' (or with an imaginary pencil), and with the wrist of his writing hand resting against the desk as when writing, they do pushing and pulling exercises. In this way the children learn to realize that it is by finger-movements and not grosser hand movements that the differences between the letters are made.

7 In their newsprint books and with large soft pencils they attempt to draw circles, 1 – 2 cm in diameter, several on top of each other, without lifting the pencil from the paper. Several such circles are drawn. Then a row of single circles is attempted, as a copy of the teacher's circles on the blackboard.

The children are taught that these circles must be:

(a) round, that is, like an orange, not like an apple, a potato or an egg:

(b) joined so that the join does not show;

(c) quickly done, with the hand relaxed;

(d) started at the top right-hand side. Upside down 'saucers' begun from the right are good practice for this. To do consecutive ones the child moves his hand to the right and his pencil makes a right to left upside down saucer. These can later be turned into letters.

These activities lead into the first stage of pattern-making, or they prepare each child's mind and hand for any of the other stages.

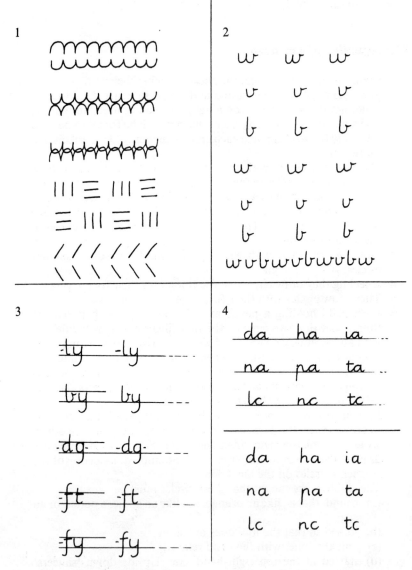

Figure 3.1   Handwriting: 1. Patterns; 2. Example of part of letter-formation worksheet; 3. Example of part of worksheet for practising relative heights of letters and their positioning on a line; 4. Examples of parts of two worksheets to teach how letters are joined

Patterns (Stage One)

The children can either continue in pencil or use felt markers, or use chalk on the teacher's blackboard. Small hand blackboards are not really big enough for the children to practise on. Their size limits too much the freedom which should be given to the hand and therefore stunts fluency. As the children become more advanced, other writing patterns are added, and later, substituted for this first one. The most important are shown (see Fig 3.1.1).

They can be repeated next to the original and the page can be turned upside down. Sometimes lines are used. Although the appearance of some pairs of patterns is identical, they are done in a different way. At least three variations of each can be obtained. Still more patterns can be made using straight lines, vertical, horizontal and diagonal.

The next stage of each handwriting lesson can be based on variations of these. Gradually the preliminaries are speeded up, and more advanced patterns replace simpler ones.

Formation of letters (Stage Two)

According to the ability of the children and when they can do each pattern fluently, the formation of the 26 letters is taught in groups: *o e c; u i l; a d q; m n p h; w v b; r; j y g; z x; t i l; f s k*: that is, letter-groups based on common directions of hand movements.

The first letters are all based on the original 'o'. They are harder to learn than those in some other groups. But this formation leads to more frequently used letters and, having mastered these, the children have a well deserved sense of achievement. They are eager to learn more and because they find many later groups easier, their ability accumulates, and soon all are learnt. During the learning of the first group it is emphasized that all letters (except of course 'e' and 'd') are begun at the top. This helps to establish the habit before the child is tempted to begin letters 'm', 'n', 'p' and 'h' from the bottom. Also it must be stressed that the middle of the vertical stroke in the 'f' is a straight line. The 'f' is a natural transition from the straight letters to the curly 's'. Children should not be worried if they cannot do 's'. Extra preliminary practice can be given by tracing on the blackboard a large 'lazy eight', that is, an eight on its side (∞). If traced several times in a continuous line in each direction every possible writing curve is practised. The most difficult letter to learn is 'r'. There is no short cut to it. Children who find this or any other letter particularly difficult to form are helped by finger-tracing letters cut into lino-blocks (about 75 mm square with small letters about 40 mm high) or on sandpaper letters.

Handwriting is taught as a separate skill from others with which it is used later. This is important. A child does not necessarily need to know what he is writing while he learns to form 'o e c', and other groups of letters. Some children need to be talked through the method of forming each new letter, and to learn to talk it through themselves. One child says 'over and up and/down and up' as he writes an 'a' or 'd'; another says 'down up/over up/over up' for an 'm'. Teachers know which children can tolerate chanting the phonic sound of each line of letters they write. This is useful for beginning to grasp the concept of phonic spelling, but the main goal of handwriting must be kept clear. And it is important to be aware of the relationship of the letter being practised, to the child's name. If her name is Sheila, the association of the sound for 's' alone, with the letter 's' is confusing. If his name is Christopher, he may wonder why the letter 'f' for which he is saying the sound 'f' is not in his name. Children's names mean so much to them at this stage that they should not be interfered with.

As each lesson progresses, each child works at his own speed. Although he must try hard to aim at a good result, this need not be perfected before practice with the next letter has begun. The grouping of letters ensures continuing interest and avoids boredom. As each letter is being learnt a few words containing the letter or letters can be copied. But the child should write only words which are phonically regular according to the primary phonic rules (i.e. one letter/one sound). Since there are few such words at the beginning of the vocabulary it is not easy to compose suitable sentences. But in early handwriting lessons it is more important to show how letters make words than how words make sentences. For this purpose the nouns are more useful than the other words.

Although it is possible for children to learn letter-formation from the repeated copying of one letter or letter-group displayed on the blackboard or written in their newsprint books, it is more efficiently done if they are provided with wide sheets of letters. These can be traced or written over, and other letters written between them both horizontally and vertically (see Figure 3.1.2). Final serifs are taught during the formation stage, on two major groups of letters, to ease the later joining stage, i.e. 'a d h i k l m n p u'; and 'b o v w' (see Figure 3.1.4 and 3.1.2).

Capital letters and figures are taught in the same way, but probably not until the formation of most lower-case letters is thoroughly mastered.

Relative heights of letters and positioning on line (Stage Three)

Although some children are worried by lines on the paper, others need 'targets' from the start, in the form of widely spaced lines, as this seems to help them to control their pencils. For these children the freedom of a blank sheet of paper is overwhelming.

But all children must be given wide-lined paper on which to practise the relative sizes and positions of the letters. Those who find difficulty in keeping on the line can be given an extra piece of paper to put under each line as they reach it. It must be moved further down for the long letters. When tall letters, 'l, d, h, b, k' first occur emphasis is laid on the comparative sizes of the short and tall letters. When 't' occurs near 'h' or 'l', it is pointed out that it is slightly shorter than the other tall letters and its cross is level with the top of the small letters. If this is learnt now, wrong habits do not have to be corrected later in the child's handwriting career. There should always be a small space between each tall letter and the line above it.

First, letters are copied in four groups:

1 a c e i m n o r s u v w x:
2 b d h k l: t which is slightly shorter
   (NB: All capital letters and numbers are in this group)
3 g j p q y z:
4 f

Then one from each of two groups are combined in pairs and repeated (see Figure 3.1.3).

On prepared sheets, double-line ruling is used. But the top guide-line fades out towards the end of the line. Some teachers suggest that the bottom line fades too. More responsibility for height differences is placed on the writer. At this stage some of the commonest uses of capital letters are practised at the beginning of a few words.

Spacing must also be emphasized here. Children should now be able to write on narrower lines (at least 1 cm.) Then horizontal spacing is emphasized. Letters within a word should almost touch each other. But words should be separated by a space at least as big as one letter.

Some children need to be taught that if they reach the end of their line before the end of the line being copied, they begin a new one and do not try the impossible task of squeezing too many letters into too small a space. Conversely, some must also be taught to fill up each line on their paper when copying a simple paragraph. There is not much opportunity to emphasize this until the stage when they are tracing and copying for fluency's sake.

Joined writing (Stage Four)

It is now a simple task for the child to transfer from unjoined to joined writing. Seven groups of letter-endings and nine groups of letter-beginnings have been made into a 'matrix', to produce all possible joins. In this way the various methods of joining letter-pairs can be practised separately. Care has been taken to exclude letter-pairs which rarely appear in English. It is possible to teach the most important of these joins by using only the letter-pairs which form words or common digraphs. Further practice in joining can be given by selecting pairs which are reversible, e.g. '-at' as in 'cat', 'ta-', as in 'tap'. When joins are practised in words, only short words should be used.

Time given to teaching joining is well spent, as it allows the teacher to concentrate later on other types of errors, i.e. arising from less mechanical and more representational skills of writing words and sentences. Point out that dots on 'i's and 'j's and crosses on 't's are added later and that all words without 'g', 'j', 'y', 'z', 'x' and 'f' in initial or medial position are one continuous line. As with formation and heights, joining is learnt more efficiently from prepared sheets. Joined letter-pairs are traced, and immediately the same letter-pairs are presented unjoined, for the child to trace or copy joined (see Figure 3.1.4).

Fluency (Stage Five)

When writing becomes fairly fluent children can try to write straight with no lines at all, but they should be allowed to choose whether they continue to do so or not, as wavy lines of handwriting may undermine the confidence which the child has gained so far.

Short passages of prose taken from wall stories and written by the teacher in pencil, can be traced quickly to encourage fluency and then copied immediately from the original onto lines in writing books. This activity has more influence on the development of a child's handwriting than most people realize. And although the results are similar, there is a greater opportunity for individuality as increased fluency earlier encourages it to develop sooner.

Conclusion

The more quickly a child can learn the rudiments of legible handwriting, the sooner he is equipped with one of the most essential tools for making progress in the learning of written language; this in turn is a vital component of the system which, for a young language disordered child, leads towards the goal of effective spoken communication.

4 Language through signing: Paget–Gorman Signed Speech

History of its introduction into the curriculum

'Signing?!' we exclaimed in the early 60s. 'Using signing with children who are not deaf?! Unthinkable!! Not even worth considering . . .' But a few months went by, and we were still considering the question. Many children were bringing their own gestures with them, which they had been using for their social survival. Decoding these signs relied heavily on the interpreters' familiarity with the commonest ideas communicated by individual children, and on a degree of inspired guessing. 'Aeroplane' and 'bird' and 'fly', for instance, shared one sign. So did 'hear' and 'listen'. We considered the possibility of using British Sign Language. But we still shared with many others the traditional and prejudiced misconception that manual systems are used for communication only by adults with a severe hearing loss. We knew groups of such users were proficient in speedy communication with each other. The natural non-verbal clues which accompanied their manual signs clarified meanings still further. The quality of their conversation paralleled that of normal speakers. And most manual systems were languages in their own right. They seemed to comprise multi-faceted concepts, and to be adaptable for international use. Communication was effective, and although a language was present, it was not one that could be matched word for word with our grammatically inflected English language. The use of this type of language was exclusive to deaf adults themselves, and to their closest hearing associates.

Once again we decided not to introduce signing into the curriculum. The children were not deaf. But they still had severe disorders of language. And it was then that we first heard of Paget. We found that Paget–Gorman Signed Speech (then still known as the Paget Sign Language) was used in only a few schools, by children who all had three handicapping conditions: hearing loss, cerebral palsy, and mental retardation.

But some remediators in other schools reported that they had tried to learn the system, but had failed to make use of it. They convinced us that it was too complex, being able to represent every word in a sentence such as 'I thought you would have known that the dog had not been given his dinner yet'. This level of production was approaching another extreme. Grammatical word-endings we needed, and signs for closed-class words. But none of our children would ever need to express such an advanced concept using such complex language structures. Besides, if the system were difficult to learn, how should we be able to teach it to the children? This time we rejected not only the sign system which proved later to fit our children's needs exactly, but also the whole idea of using manual signing as an aid to teaching spoken language!

Still later, we heard about Paget in yet another context. It was being used effectively in a school for children with both hearing and sight problems. But it is a visual system. How could these children with poor sight in addition to poor hearing benefit from a communication system which relied on the user being able to see? Out of sheer curiosity this school was visited. There Paget had been grasped as an indispensable teaching tool by an experienced teacher, whose enthusiasm led her to carry the heavy Paget manual wherever she went. She decoded the instructions for signs as the children needed them, she signed them expansively, and the children made use of what little sight they had to take full advantage of this key to an environment which became gradually less confusing. Children with no speech at all, nor any ability in writing, were communicating with their hands. How could we withhold such a system from our children with severe language disorders who needed it so much? So we decided to try it first with the group of children with receptive problems.

The System

One of the fundamental principles of the system is the grouping of signs for words with related meanings around 37 basic signs, the descriptions of which are based on 21 standard hand postures. Once these are thoroughly grasped, the decoding of others' signing becomes simpler. A 'position' sign is the basis for all the preposition signs; a 'water' sign is used in different locations and movement-directions for 'rain', 'snow', 'river', and 'sea'; upon 'think' are based the related signs for 'understand', 'remember', and 'forget'.

The semantic system is so logical that when some signs are produced, further paired signs can be guessed: from the signs for 'male', 'father', 'brother' and 'boy', can be deduced the parallel signs for 'female', 'mother', 'sister' and 'girl'. From two or three signs for specific days of the week, or specific months, others can be assumed; and 'pretty', 'sweet', 'kind' and their opposites are modifications of 'good' and 'bad'. Signs for 'morning' and 'breakfast' are similar, in the same way as 'afternoon' and 'lunch'. The differences are made by the modifying hand indicating 'sun' (in 'morning' and 'afternoon') or 'food' (in 'breakfast' and 'lunch'). There are also distinct differences between signs for 'see', 'look', and 'watch'; and for 'sound', 'noise', and 'noisy'; and other groups of two or three signs with related meanings.

Another major feature of the system is the inclusion of signs for grammatical word-endings. This distinguishes it from the sign languages whose main role is communication, and which have limited means, or

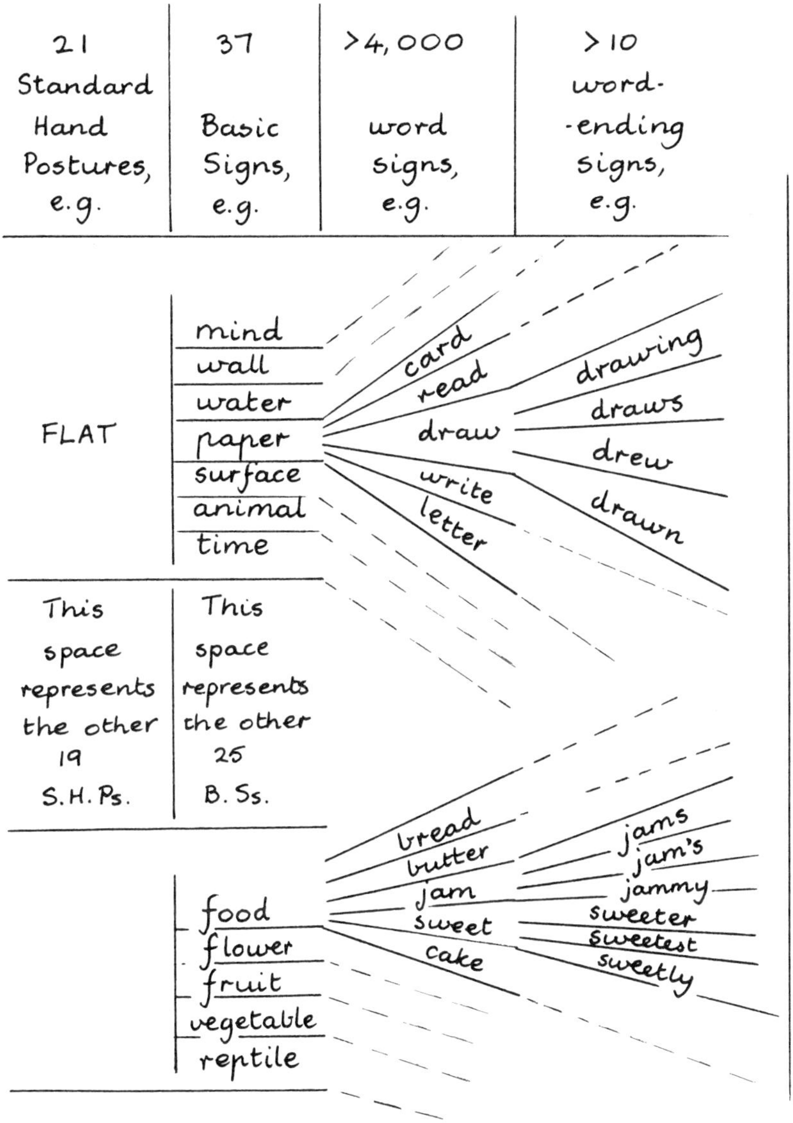

21 Standard Hand Postures, e.g.	37 Basic Signs, e.g.	>4,000 word signs, e.g.	>10 word-ending signs, e.g.
FLAT	mind wall water paper surface animal time	card read draw write letter	drawing draws drew drawn
This space represents the other 19 S.H.Ps.	This space represents the other 25 B.Ss.		
	food flower fruit vegetable reptile	bread butter jam sweet cake	jams jam's jammy sweeter sweetest sweetly

Figure 4.1   The structure of Paget-Gorman Signed Speech

none at all, for teaching syntactic structure. To nouns can be added a plural sign (changing 'house' to 'houses', and 'man' to 'men', for example); a possessive –'s sign (which differentiates between more than one person or animal, and the possession of an item by that person, that is, the difference between 'the babies', and 'the baby's' or even 'the babies' ' dinner); and the –y which converts a noun to an adjective, such as 'sunny', or 'watery'. To verb stems can be added the continuous '-ing'; the third person singular '-s', as in 'jumps' and 'eats'; a sign to mark the past tense; and another to mark the past participle or passive. There is a sign for every *modal* verb, such as 'can', 'must', and 'should'. Adjective-signs can be followed with the superlative '-est', the comparative '-er' and the '—ly' which converts an adjective to an adverb.

To complete the syntactic power of the system, there is a separate sign for every closed-class word: all the question-words, conjunctions, pronouns, noun determiners, prepositions, adverbs, and 'not'. 'And why could she not find the dogs very easily?' is a brief example of the potential use of these types of signs. They are indispensable to any group of remediators who are using the system as one of the media for teaching syntactic usage.

The system comprises manual signs for more than 4,000 lexical words. Some of the commonest signs are made with one hand only, as in 'I am happy'. Others are made with both hands, as in 'They were sitting'. Some are static, as in 'Think of it'. But others are moving: the hand remains in a stationary position, while the fingers move, as in 'the fire'; or one of the two hands involved in making the sign moves, as in 'cut his bread'; in a few signs, such as 'work with either swimmer', both hands move simultaneously; and in still fewer they move together, as in 'bring their bags'. Either hand can be used for making the one-handed signs, and for making the movement in the one-moving-hand signs, but most signers choose their dominant hand.

About one in seven of the frequently used nouns, adjectives and verbs can be understood by a non-user of the system. Having learned to recognize the two closed-class signs 'the' and 'is', she can readily decode 'The house is hot', 'the dog is cold', 'shut your eyes', and 'open the book'. Having learned 'can' and 'must', a newcomer understands the complete sentences, 'can you hear the telephone?', and 'you must stop and look and listen'.

A further attraction to this system for use with children who are likely to need to make several hundred different signs, is that the instructions for making every sign are easily read and understood, once the simple abbreviation method is grasped. Part of this, and underlying many of the lexical signs, is a system of 21 standard hand postures. By using these, much unnecessary repetition in the instruction manual is eliminated. And, together with a few more specific meanings of words like 'shake' and 'vibrate', and adherence to well defined meanings of words like 'own' and 'other', 'in' and 'out', standard hand postures are an essential feature of the way in which the instructions are given. Well motivated, careful and logical adults cannot fail to make the same signs as each other when following the same instructions. Further instructions can be written in the same way for any additional signs which are agreed upon. There is no need for photographs, and the only hand-drawings provided are those of the standard hand postures and basic signs.

Some specific uses of the system

Once a remediator has grasped the essential principles on which the system is based, and begins to use it, she gradually discovers an increasing number of uses for it. General recommendations on methods of use are few, as they vary according to the specific needs of individual users, and even according to differences in the situation of the same user. For purposes of the description of some of these uses it seems simpler to make a distinction between attention, communication and language.

The use of the system for attention training

One of the important prerequisites for communication is the control of attention. This must be gained and held if any transmission of meaning is to take place. The visual nature of any sign system is an attraction in itself. It is as much more salient and perceptible than any auditory–vocal language system. Hands are bigger than lips, and have so many more parts, all of which can be moved separately. A moving hand in front of a very distractable child attracts his attention; and, once attracted, it is easier to keep by signing than by talking alone. Differences between the hands' movements are many, due to their directions and sizes, and the combinations of these. Optimum differences between those signs which represent the most frequent words and concepts result in the speediest decoding. At a more advanced level, when a much greater sign-vocabulary is known, decoding may be more difficult. This applies not only to the receivers' memories, but also to the signers' accuracy.

The use of the system for teaching communication

In some children it is a physical difficulty which hinders their acquisition of spoken communication skills; in others it is a hearing loss, or low intelligence, or specific language disorders. Others show no desire to communicate. When a child's disorders of language appear to derive from more than one of these factors, it is often difficult for a remediator to decide how to start to help him. A manual sign system has proved to be a useful tool in motivating a child to communicate; and also to help others to overcome difficulties based on their physical handicap, hearing loss, or low intelligence. It is particularly useful for those children who have the maximum desire to communicate, but whose specific language disorder hinders their spoken language development, despite no visible physical handicap, intact hearing, and average non-verbal intelligence. Such a child may have very poor auditory skills, but he has the ability to learn visually. So teaching methods must make maximum use of this positive factor. Our main purpose initially in introducing the sign system was to provide a communication tool for the children with severe receptive language disorders. So, for the benefit of the minority of children, all the others learned it too. It soon became apparent that they were learning it far more quickly than the adults. Even those children who learned it for the sake of the minority regarded it as an enjoyable code-cracking activity. In six months it had become a common language currency. The children with receptive disorders used Paget signs in every situation in the school, with child care officers, speech therapists and teachers. Their parents wanted to use the system, too, and they learned its basic essentials at a weekend intensive course. The parents of two children with expressive disorders reported enthusiastically that during their holiday they were being taught by their children a system which they had previsouly known nothing about. The child-teachers were just as proud of their own achievement.

A young child whose specific language problem has been recognized early profits from being encouraged to take part in a signing environment. A child who reaches school age before any concentrated attempt is made to teach him language must eventually be taught to read and write, as a visual aid to spoken language, as well as for its own sake. Compared to speech, the tools for this are cumbersome, and bring with them additional difficulties relating to hand–eye coordination and hand control. How much simpler it is to begin without a writing tool, and to use hands alone. Such a communication system is more convenient, more salient, and more flexible than a written system.

1 Initial communication
A child with a receptive disorder who has previously been forced to rely on pointing, screaming, leading by the hand, and largely on the goodwill and intuition of his parents, suddenly discovers Paget. He finds himself in an environment in which, if he waves his hands about, he can get what he wants. He eagerly demands to be shown the signs for 'bread', 'salt', 'bike', and so on. He finds they work like magic. He even learns new concepts like 'wait', and the signs to represent them. He has found a key which he had not known he needed.

There are a few children who need to be nudged towards this discovery. The sign which any child can be forced into using is the one for 'toilet'. Its frequency proves its value. It teaches the concept of signing and many other signs follow, the most motivating ones being those representing different types of food.

2 Overcoming shyness

A child whose speech has rarely been understood is often afraid to initiate communication. It is easier for him to take life as it comes than to endure the frustration of failure. He is introduced to Paget. At first he fears this in the same way as speech. But his teacher signs useful phrases with him. He learns to complete the ones she begins, and gradually becomes more confident in his own signing ability. Then he uses the signed phrases in appropriate real situations. Later he also becomes more confident in his own ability to speak, and will eventually find himself able to dispense with the signs.

3 Breaking through blocks in conversation

A child who had a severe speech difficulty improved so much that he can hold an interesting conversation. But he comes to a word that the listener cannot understand. Several times he repeats the word, to no avail. The listener asks him to sign it, which he does. The conversation can now continue.

4 An aid to lip-reading

A child with a receptive language disorder, with or without a hearing loss, tries to decode what his teacher says. He understands that he must 'put the pencil', but where must be put it? When his teacher speaks without signing, he makes a wild guess, and puts the pencil in a box. But she is not satisfied. She accompanies her words 'in your desk' with the three signs, and the message becomes clear. He knows she means 'in', not 'on' or 'under'; 'your' and not 'my'; 'desk', and not 'box'. Gradually he learns to associate common lip-read patterns with their appropriate signs, and his lip-reading improves.

5 Reading

When a teacher 'listens' to a language disordered child reading, it is helpful when the child signs words which the teacher would otherwise not understand. Other children find that signing helps them to understand. They read, signing and speaking simultaneously. They seem to enjoy the power in their hands that conquers the print in the book.

The use of the system for teaching the structure of language

Over the two years following the introduction of Paget–Gorman Signed Speech to the school, the communicative purpose was retained. At the same time, a broader purpose was being discovered. The children with primarily receptive disorders now had a tool for learning the structure of language. This tool was now being shared by the children with primarily expressive disorders. The existence of signs not only for every noun, verb and adjective, but also for every word which cements these content words to each other, together with word-endings, turned primitive communication into language. Remediators found that, because signs for all these words were available, they were more readily included in running conversation, making this more natural than it was before signing accompanied speech. Children understood the feeling of the meanings of the signs, and incorporated them into their own communication. Differences between meanings of words and signs such as 'now' and 'later', which could not be explained, were learned by constant usage in context. All prepositions were distinguishable. So were all pronouns, which are among the hardest words for specifically language disordered children to learn. PGSS provides differences between gender, number and case. So distinctions can be made in sign between 'him' and 'her', between 'him' and 'them', and between 'him' and 'he'. Paget also provides differences between all parts of the verb 'to be', i.e. *is, am, are, was, were, be, being, been.* 'Is', 'am' and 'was' are shown with one finger each sliding along one part of the body; for 'are' and 'were' two fingers are used. The past tense of 'was' and 'were' is shown by the other hand, the 'time'-hand, moving backwards. The same movement shows the past tense of all verbs. For the future tense, the word 'will' is represented by the time-hand moving forwards.

The children are not taught to understand or use words which in themselves describe language. So a child who has realized the existence of the past tense is not able to ask in spoken words, 'What is the past tense of the verb 'to sit?' And how do you spell it? But he can do better than that. He can sign 'sit' and then the past tense sign, and present the teacher with pencil and paper on which to write 'sat'.

And the signs for each of the grammatical '–s's are distinct from each other. Sentences like 'The cat eats the dogs' biscuits' and 'Let's use yours', when spoken or written, must produce some '–s-confusion' in a child's mind. When they are signed, all the signs for final '–s' are different. Gradually the meanings of these different uses are absorbed. A child who wrote about 'the birds's feet' and 'the cars's wheels' proved not only that he understood the necessity for both the plural and the possessive '–s's, but also that Paget is more accurate than English!

Word order
Word order in Paget is identical to word order in English, or any other language. No words are excluded, and there is a one-to-one relationship between spoken words and signs. So any sentence can be signed in the normal way. But there is no need to sign complete sentences to a very young specifically language disordered child. Signing can be used alongside any language scheme or teaching method. If a child can, for any reason, be expected to understand or produce only two signs in a sequence, then there is no need to present him with more than two matching spoken words and signs. Other remediators may want to sign more, or less, than they say. Paget is a tool and can be used as the remediator wishes. But we

can never expect a child to sign at a more advanced level than that which he sees.

Basic signs

These brings some semantic order into the child's confused world. At mealtimes the basic sign for food is often used. It is the basis for bread, butter, marmalade and milk, etc. The other hand differentiates between these by showing a slicing movement for bread, a spoon's action for marmalade and a teat-pulling action for milk. The child's aim is to procure what he wants to eat and drink. But there is a bonus. Without even trying he learns that there is a similarity between the three items. When he has learned still more food signs, the modifying second hand is removed from them all. What is left? Food. He has learned the name of a category of objects. The same is true, at a more advanced stage, of other signs, such as 'position' and 'time'. All classification tasks, and especially this kind, are very difficult for language disordered children. They often find the words for prepositions hard to learn. But the Paget sign for 'position' provides a common reference point. The other hand shows the precise relationship between the subject being positioned and the object on which it is positioned.

Speech accompanies signing

For communication purposes, adults and children ideally sign and speak simultaneously. Children see the syntactic structure of language in the large three-dimensional area in front of the signer's body. This is more salient than the smaller lip-read pattern which they will later use to reinforce what they hear, in the same way as hearing people do. But there are rare situations in which speech is not always used to accompany signs. Signing a very short simple story with no spoken clues encourages visual attention. The children attend because they want to know the story, and simultaneously they are being presented with examples of the same simple structures which they are learning in reading and writing lessons. Some children whisper the words as they decode the signs. This is usually followed by a short question and answer session. It is simpler to use speech at this stage, with or without signing.

A sign can be used by a speech therapist as a quick stimulus for the child's discrimination or production of a word. It is quicker than searching for pictures. For example, a child looks at an array of three cards, each with a letter which represents the final sound of a word. The therapist signs the word and the child must point to the card with the letter which stands for the final sound in the signed word.

Misconceptions dispersed

At a time when sign systems are being compared with each other by so many groups of professionals for use with so many groups of users, Gorman's observations (1983) are not only relevant: they are vital.

PGSS does not replace speech
'Although effective grammatical communication can be achieved by using the PGSS entirely in a manual form it is intended to be used simultaneously with spoken communication'.

It appears that some comparisons are being made on the premise that signing replaces speech. This should not be its aim. If speech is not the ultimate goal, then of course it is not necessary to use a syntactic system. Basic primitive communication can take place with body movement and facial expression, but this is not grammatically acceptable language. Immediate meaning can be conveyed by strings of single open-class words or signs, but it is the word-endings and closed class words which add important details of number, gender, tense, degree, probability, etc., etc. Everyone, except those with an extremely low intelligence, needs to express and understand the modifications which these variations allow.

The PGSS is useful, secondarily for communication itself, and primarily as a two-way 'language bridge': between the intention and the spoken expression of the intended communication; and between the perception of another person's expression and its transmission into meaning; the bridge itself comprises an association of spoken and signed language, resulting in effective communication.

It has been said by theorists that the encouragement of signing decreases the possibility of speech. But children with specific language disorders prove that in practice the opposite is true. As they use their hands to make useful signs, tension in their speech musculature is reduced, they become less afraid of trying to speak, and so it becomes easier for them.

In addition to the small visual aid of lip-reading employed naturally by most people, they have a larger visual aid of two hands, moving in a large three-dimensional area in front of the signer's body. They can see language structure more easily, and it becomes more salient in a similar way to that of a large-print book for a new reader.

PGSS signs are discarded when no longer needed
Dr Gorman continues: . . 'manual signs are spontaneously discarded when they have served their purpose'. Here is another important fact of a specifically language disordered child's life. Signing is a means to an end, and the end is spoken language. It is a semantic and syntactic link between primitive incomprehensible vocalization to meaningful and effective speech. As an adult he has no need to live in a world of people with hearing problems. So he has no need to learn their signs. Even the minority about

whom this is not true have not found transition to another system difficult.

PGSS is not difficult to learn
Many people argue that the PGSS is too difficult to learn. Too difficult for whom? Children with specific language disorders rarely fail to learn it. They cannot afford not to do so, and most of them have no difficulty in acquiring a basic vocabulary of signs. As in any learning, the older the learner, the more difficulty is experienced. It is quite possible for any well motivated adult to learn the basic essentials of the PGSS in one day. If he has the opportunity to put his knowledge to immediate use, his motivation increases, and he can continue to teach himself the signs he needs from the current total of over 4,000. No other sign system has a comparable wealth of resources readily available in one handbook. And the system's foundation of basic signs makes it so logical that this in itself is a further incentive to learn more. The instructions can be interpreted as easily as a simple knitting pattern or a DIY instruction book.

Degrees of accuracy
The large number of words for which there are PGSS signs is one of the reasons for the 'precise verbal instructions' in the PGSS manual. Any two people who have become efficient, through practice, in reading these instructions, will produce exactly the same sign. It was Dr Gorman himself who devised the method to describe the signs in such detail. It is important that remediators learn to sign as accurately as possible, in order to give a good model to the children. It is, of course, impracticable to demand such accuracy from the children themselves. The most frequent signs have enough distinctive properties that they cannot be confused with each other. One of the worst exceptions to this statement is the pair of signs for 'colour' and 'many'. But if the instructions for these are adhered to properly, there is no need for confusion. And children find less difficulty in practice than adults estimate in theory. The PGSS at this level is much less complex than the similarities between word-pairs in spoken English, like 'I' and 'eye', with which the children successfully contend.

Conclusion

In order to achieve the goal of more effective communication, it is desirable to teach all aspects of a commonly accepted language – its uses, its meanings, its grammatical structures, its phonology, and the ways in which these aspects can be encoded into writing and print. The uses and basic meanings of language can be learnt from any manual sign system. But more specific meanings and grammatical structures can be taught only through one which is specially designed mainly for this purpose. Some remediators consider that the group of children with specific language disorders is the one for whom Sir Richard Paget was asked to devise his system, described by Prebendary Albert Smith as 'a small group of children in schools for the deaf who were unable to learn from the teaching methods currently being used by teachers of the deaf' (1934). The corollary of this is that no other system provides for the special needs of children with severe specific language disorders. One common misconception about the PGSS is that in order to use the system you must be deaf! This highlights the lack of public awareness about the existence of children who are specifically language disordered.

Many speech therapists, child care workers and teachers of children with specific language disorders have learnt from experience that the PGSS is the best signing tool for their children. It has all the advantages of the other systems, and many additional ones. The power of a semantically logical foundation, and the availability of signs for all English closed-class words, and all grammatical word-endings, is increased still further by signs for prefixes and suffixes, such as 'un–' and '–er' which converts a verb to a noun, as in 'swimmer'.

Remediators of children who have language handicaps which are attributed to a definite cause such as hearing loss or low intelligence have a very difficult task to decide which of the many sign systems to employ. For what purpose do they need to use one at all – for teaching the elements of grammar, or for teaching a basic means of communication, or both? Presumably there are deaf children who can learn to communicate grammatically with no help from any sign system. There are others who cannot. Presumably there are children with moderate learning difficulties whose remediators have decided, for whatever reason, that it is not worth giving them a signing tool.

The remark 'He doesn't need Paget' is very suspicious if 'he' happens to have a specific language disorder. It is rare to find such a child who doesn't need the system to help him in at least one of the ways described and usually it is found that he needs it for more than one. It improves the quality of language comprehension and production, and thus of communication skills. When it is given a fair chance, how can it fail?

5 Language through speaking: A remediation programme based on LARSP

The main goal of all remediators is to work towards the improvement of the quality of the children's understanding and use of spoken language. To this end all adults concerned with them are constantly considering specific ways of helping children through barriers, over hurdles, and up the gentle slopes of progress.

It is difficult to use the same linguistic sample as a basis for the analysis of every aspect of a child's expressive skills. A few attempts have been made to devise procedures for analysing two or more aspects, and the links between them: but the Language Assessment and Remediation Screening Procedure (LARSP), devised by Crystal, Fletcher and Garman (1976), emphasizes the grammatical aspect. This does not imply that it totally disregards other aspects. It is a suitable procedure for classroom teachers to understand and use, as it is practicable for them to be among the key remediators of immature grammatical disability, leaving speech therapists to spend more time on the remediation of disorders of speech. It is of course essential for parents and all professional adults concerned with each child to cooperate in encouraging acceptable ways of using grammar and speech to communicate meaning.

The verbal comprehension of young school-age children with expressive language disorders, measured on the Reynell scale, is on average one year below that of their chronological age. But on the expressive scale, which includes three aspects of expression (language structure, vocabulary and content), their language ages range between 18 months and five years. Both the comprehension and expressive ability of the children with severe receptive disorders are even more limited.

The ways in which these children express themselves spontaneously range from gross manual gestures and/or grunts, to speech which – though its meaning can usually by understood – is inappropriate when compared to the children's intelligence and non-verbal competence. When it is encoded into a written form, it is even less acceptable. It is composed of strings of open-class words and a few prepositions and possessives. They are usually in the right order so the utterances are semantically viable. But pronouns are substituted for each other, with object-pronouns predominating; there is no implicit tense distinction; most noun-determiners are omitted, and so are all the parts of the verb *to be*. Negatives and conjunctions are rare.

Possible reasons for these deviations are that the children are intelligent and aware enough to want to express interesting information about people and things around them, but have not yet been able to understand the relativity of 'I' and 'you'; they are uninterested in the differences between male and female, and are unable to generalize the difference between the subject and the object of the verb; there has been little need for them to distinguish the past or future from the present. Because ownership is important, so are the words *mine, my,* and *yours, your,* but the relative position of objects distinguished by *this* and *that* is not important, and the subtle distinctions between demonstratives and articles, and between the definite and indefinite articles even less so. The 'is-ness' of an object is so obvious that it is not worth remarking upon with the use of *is* or any of its counterparts. Perhaps because these children have a positive outlook on life, negatives are seldom necessary. Because the concepts of causality, purpose and conditionality are not yet formed, conjunctions are not needed.

LARSP aims to provide a framework of cumulative syntactic patterns, as a foundation for working primarily on the grammatical aspect of language. Using this, the average range among young school-age language disordered children is between Stages I and II, estimated by the authors of LARSP at 'grammatical ages' between nine months and two years.

LARSP analysis

First, a sample of each child's spoken language is obtained, of about 15 minutes' duration. It is possible to use a simple elicitation procedure as a rough guide to progress, but this can only supplement, and not be substituted for, the complete analysis of the initial spontaneous sample. These utterances are transcribed, and, when analysed, examples of each identifiable structure are counted, and the numbers recorded on the form. Each child's grammatical profile is studied, and children are grouped according to similarities between these. (NB: Greater detail about methods of sampling, transcription, analysis, profiling and interpretation is given in '*Working with LARSP* (Crystal, 1979, pp.154–60). An example of a case study is also provided there, and further details of an elicitation procedure.)

Remediation based on LARSP

Remediation must be planned to achieve the greatest good for the greatest number of children possible. Time never allows for two adults to work with one child, and rarely in the classroom for one adult with one child. The most economical arrangement is to divide each class of nine children into three or four groups of two or three children, whose profiles match each other as nearly as possible. The adults leading the groups are the class teacher and the speech therapist, who remediate the two most difficult groups; and one other teacher and the teachers' aide. Each group meets for three 20-minute sessions every week, and remediation is brisk and business-like.

The overall goal is to straighten each child's profile, before proceeding to further stages. Each remediator has a long-term plan, and the gaps in the profile provide a ready made list of goals for each child. They are ordered with the following criteria:

Clause structure should be at least as advanced as phrase structure and word-endings; phrase structure is next in importance, and word-endings the least.

Elicitation of statements should precede that of questions. (It must be borne in mind that the child who asks the initial questions of the teacher who models the replies is taking the part of the second adult in the ideal situation. The teacher's aim in asking him to do this is not to provide practice for him, but a stimulus for her own response.)

While it is understood that children with normally developing language use pronouns, past tenses, past participles and noun plurals incorrectly before generalizing the rules or their exceptions to correct them, we believe that children with expressive difficulties of any kind should be given correct models and taught to copy, practise and remember them at a comparatively much earlier stage. It has been found in grammatical and other areas that once an error has been established because it has been ignored or because no attempt has been made to correct it, it is extremely difficult to replace it with the acceptable version. This means that, particularly in the items mentioned, more practice than at first would seem necessary should be given to these children, in order that they overlearn each item rather than risk its being forgotten when new ones are introduced and supersede it.

For some children and in some situations, it may not be necessary to make a profile at all. The first step is to teach a few *intransitive verbs*. A child to whom some are already available can be taught the words or signs for two or more people, and simple subject–verb sequences can be practised. A child who finds the next steps relatively easy is not wasting time. He is gradually absorbing more about the concept of the method being used. The time will come when he finds a task difficult. This is when he begins to learn grammar systematically. He has to work harder. He enjoys the challenge. Further practice makes him more proficient. The reduction of clues makes the exercise more realistic. Before he incorporates the practised structure into his spontaneous production, he will have begun to practise another structure which had not previously been available. The process is like the waves rolling on to the sea shore. Each structure being used spontaneously is being closely followed by another which can be produced in a practice session when clues have been removed. In turn this is being followed by yet another which the child finds difficulty in producing, even when all the clues are present.

Although it is theoretically possible to put this remediation scheme into practice without a working knowledge of the Paget–Gorman Sign System and Remedial Syntax, it would be much more difficult, and not as effective. Manual signs from other systems could be substituted, but it is essential that separate signs for grammatical word-endings are available. Other ideographic systems could be used for the visual non-word referents on the cards, to be described later. Other colour-pattern coding systems could be used, but preferably only those with eight separate colours for nouns, noun determiners, verbs, adjectives, pronouns, verb particles, prepositions and conjunctions.

Teaching materials

The grammar we teach must be semantically based. The meaningful elements in a simple sentence must permute in as many ways as possible, and their number increase: the quality of phrase structure must be improved; endings must be used to modify the meanings of open-class words, for example, 'big', 'dog', 'run'; and the possibilities of ellipsis in speech must be introduced, as in 'He's not running', 'She won't come', 'It isn't mine'.

A verb is the kernel of an acceptable clause. So the children are taught to associate manual signs and written words with a few common intransitive actions which can be linked only with a subject until prepositions are used. They are permuted with all the available subjects, that is, all the children and adults within the classroom; and soon the actions of others in the building can be described. More concentrated practice in signing and/or saying the sentences can be given with two simple sets of cards.

The teaching-material is a big pack of cards which has evolved from very small beginnings. Each coloured card is 3 inches square.

Verb cards and noun cards

On each yellow card is drawn a simple representation of the manual sign for a particular verb. A drawing of a sign is one of the ways in which a verb can be produced at random without a specific subject being present. The stem of the verb is written at the bottom of the card, so that the end of the word is flush with the right-hand edge of the card. The reason for this is that the card is placed to cover the left half of a 3" × 6" horizontal rectangle; immediately to the right of the square card the verb-ending '*ing*' has been written. In order to allow for the changes in the written form of words with single consonant or –*e* endings, the final consonant is repeated, or the –*e* is crossed out.

On each orange noun card is a simple drawing of the head of a person (man, woman, boy, girl) or animal (cat, dog, bird). The drawings of the adult heads are at the top of their squares, and the children at the bottom of theirs; the females have hair, but the males have none. The children remember these conventions very quickly, but if they do not, it does not really matter, as syntactically the differences are unimportant. Cards representing other parts of speech will be described later.

The teaching technique described with reference to the first task, the elicitation of simple statements

The teaching-sequence which follows applies to all other examples of the production of statements or their parts, at all three levels, in clauses, phrases, and words. The P in every case stands for the group of children. When P understands that people or animals can be permuted with actions, the cards are laid out on a desk in front of him. T sits opposite. Facing P is the array:

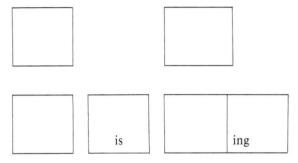

Above the two spaces are placed piles, one of human nouns, and one of intransitive verbs. When one from each pile is turned over to fill the space, a sentence appears, for example, '(The) boy is running'. But as it is accompanied by a question, one card precedes the other: the verb card is turned over before the question, '*Who is* [verb] *-ing?*' Then the noun card is turned over so that the answer can be supplied. The method of elicitation is a modified form of modelled imitation. At first the most advanced P in the group is told to ask the question, e.g. *Who is coming?* (If necessary, T can help P with the question by signing it or writing it down.) T replies, *The man is coming.* P asks the same kind of question again, this time referring to another verb-card. T answers again. When Ps have listened to answers for long enough, the rôles are reversed, and Ps in turn answer T's questions. If the question is to be *What is the* [noun] *doing?* the noun card is turned over before the question is asked: then the verb card is turned over so that the question can be answered.

The questions can if necessary be simplified to *who?* or *what. . . . doing?* The answers can be simplified to a noun/verb pattern with no *the*, no *is* and no *-ing*. With some Ps it is preferable that both question and answer utterances are complete, but the signing strings are reduced. Decisions about permutations like this can be made on the spot, according to the ability of P, and/or the expectation of T.

Plate 5.1   The sentence is being spoken and signed.

The first introduction of negativity should be in connection with present continuous verbs, though not necessarily as early as this. The type of questions changes from *who . . .?* or *. . . . doing?* to a *yes/no* type, e.g. *Is the man running?* A pile of 'yes' and 'no' cards provide the cue to the answer. If 'yes' is turned up, an extended answer is *Yes, the man in running*, or *Yes he is*, with an emphatic *is*. It should be made clear here that the subject and auxiliary are reversed in order to produce a question. At first they can be changed over but this is too cumbersome a process to do quickly. Once the principle is grasped, the word *is* can be written twice on a horizontally rectangular card. When the question is asked, the one on the right of P is covered by the subject-card. Before the spoken answer is given, the subject-card is slid over to cover the *is* on the left. The *is* card itself does not slide about if fixed to the desk with re-usable adhesive, such as Blu-tack.

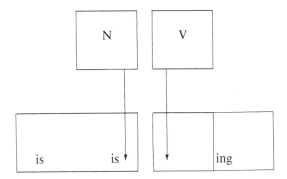

Progressions

1 Sequence of difficulty

It would be impossible to make the same definite sequence of practice designed to be suitable for every P. It is only possible to indicate progressions in each aspect. These can be dovetailed for each group of children who unknowingly dictate the next step. For instance, given a set of *quasi-transitive* verbs (such as 'eating', 'playing', 'drawing'), they can make acceptable sentences with no object. But eventually one of them completes the sentence in a different way, that is, not only with a verb but also an object, thus setting an example to the other children who usually need only a little encouragement to follow it. The way is then open for the progression from *What is the man doing?* to *What is the man eating?* and thence to *transitive verbs*, when the first question can be *What is the man making?* with the answer . . . *a car*. The second can be *What is the man doing?* with the answer . . . *making a car*. The last question *What is happening?* is answered by the complete statement *The man is making a car*.

A remediation scheme with a grammatical basis cannot fail to take semantic aspects of language into account. Speech therapists and teachers control the 'teaching' environment and materials in such a way that utterances, although imposed on children by random permutations of arrays of coloured cards, usually make sense. Pairs and trios of open-class words are combined in a simple enough way that semantic boundaries are rarely reached, and certainly need not be crossed. When the remediator presents 'the man/woman/boy/girl is eating/riding/drawing', the grammatical objects are either omitted or supplied by the children.

Most children need no visual aid for the object of the sentence, but for those who do, a blank orange card can be placed after the verb. Children at a more advanced stage enjoy having a pile of object-drawings to turn over. The object does not often relate well to the verb. But the child says whether it makes sense or not. If not, he thinks of a more suitable object. This is a useful variation if a group begins to get bored with working on the basic structure. The remediator must be sure that all the children in the group recognize inappropriate objects. Otherwise the procedure is semantically unsound.

(a) *Verbs*. The use of a main verb is vital to a clause; auxiliaries are considered at phrase level; and verb-ending modifications are among the earliest to appear in normal development. Verbs are relevant to all three sections, and of paramount importance. Once the use of *is* (phrase level) is firmly established, *are* is taught. At first, the indeterminate *they* may be used to describe any pairs or larger groups of people or animals. Then the plural pack is shuffled with the singular pack, and the alternatives *is* and *are* are shown. When names of people in the environment are used as alternatives to 'the boy', etc., a child sometimes turns up his own name. He is taught to use *am* in this context. If a child is too confused by this demand, all names of children in the group are removed before the next session, and not replaced until this extra item can be tolerated, and easily incorporated.

Some children may need extraneous clues for a full understanding of the need for the past tense (word level). So an introductory item, e.g. *last Thursday*, precedes the subject when *was* and *were* are first introduced. They can usually be taught together. The concepts of singularity and plurality have been established from *is* and *are*, and this concept of tense difference is a different aspect, which still includes singularity and plurality.

Later the time clue may be removed from the beginning of the sentence and replaced at the end. But by this time each child can choose his own time-element. This is an effective test of whether he understands the difference between past and present. Past historic forms should be introduced soon after this. As the most common verbs have irregular forms, there is no extra card with the regular *-ed* ending. Instead, another yellow card is fixed behind each verb card by a staple at the top. At the bottom of the back card is the past tense word. The first time it is introduced the new past-tense forms should be included in the question, e.g. starting with *Who ran*? rather than *What did John do*? Most children do not need to look at the past tense word in response to the first question. But when it is necessary, for example, after the second type of question, the child lifts the top card and 'reads' the past tense of a verb, and those who cannot decode it from its written or printed form in other contexts, can remember the word when they see it on the back card. Gradually each child remembers it without looking.

The future tense can be approached by the colloquial *going to*. An appropriate time phrase can be placed at the beginning of the sentence in early practice, e.g. *next week*, but later can be removed, and a self-chosen item can be added to the verb by the child. The variation *I* (or *we* or *they*) *want to* can be introduced here. Until the third person singular form of the verb is taught, no people or third person singular pronouns can be used.

Lee's (1966) sequence in her plan for *Developmental Sentence Scoring* has been used as a basis for the progression in auxiliary verbs. The next subsidiary verbs to appear are *can, will* and *may*. It is more appropriate to use these with transitive verbs, as the doubt implied when these words are used as questions is more often related to the object than the verb itself, e.g. *Can/will/may she (get the dinner)?* When the negative aspect is introduced with these verbs, the step from *can* and *not*, *will* and *not* to *can't* and *won't* follows fairly soon, at approximately the same time as the positives *could, would, should* and *might*. Later, *couldn't* and *wouldn't* are joined by *must, shall, ought to*, and *have/had/has to*. At approximately the same time comes the need for the use of *don't, didn't* and *doesn't* in negative statements. It is however important that practice in past tense forms should precede practice in *did, do* and *does* questions, which in their turn should be fully established before *didn't, don't* and *doesn't* questions are introduced.

Next comes the past participle (word level) which, in normal development, is used at roughly the same time in the present and past perfect (e.g. *I have eaten, I had eaten*). It is questionable whether the *-en* forms should be introduced before or after the forms which match the ordinary past tense. It is probably better to practise the new construction with known forms of the verb, e.g. *washed* and *painted*, then proceed to a selected group of *-en* verbs, e.g. *grown, done, given*; and finally to mix the two types.

The third person singular of the present simple tense (word level) is not in common use. It should be practised with the verbs on which it is most often used, and which are followed by fairly simple direct objects, e.g. *likes, loves, wants, uses*. The inclusion of *says, thinks, hopes*, etc. presupposes an ability to form noun-clause objects. This may be possible, especially if the introduction of the *-s* form has been delayed. When the *-s* is used easily by a group of children, its use can be generalized by occasional practices with the other verbs, but with the addition of a choice of the three adverbs *always, sometimes* and *never* in an initial or medial position, e.g. *everybody always sits*; *sometimes he eats (bananas)*; *she never makes dresses*.

The use of two auxiliaries together (phrase-level) *would be -ing, must have -en*, etc. are useful semantic starters. They almost always invite a subordinate clause. The adult can judge whether a child has internalized the meaning of a modal verb by the way in which he follows it by another phrase or clause. It is at this stage that subordinating conjunctions can be permuted along with the rest of the parts of speech. But this must be done carefully. It is usually wiser to provide a choice of conjunctions rather than a random selection. Some of the verbs can be eliminated from the pack to reduce the number of nonsense sentences. Or an unsuitable conjunction picked at random from the top of a pile can be rejected to the bottom of the pile. In the latter case, there should be several copies of each conjunction in the pile, to avoid frustration.

(b) Nouns and pronouns. These are the subjects and objects of simple sentences at clause level; they are preceded by determiners and/or possessing nouns, and/or adjectives, and/or prepositions to form noun phrases.

(c) Noun determiners. It seems in practice that *the* is the most useful determiner to introduce first, as it can be used for both singulars and plurals. For the same reason *my* and *your* can be introduced soon, probably first in the object position or before inanimate subjects. When all the subjects are singular, *this* and *that* provide interesting alternatives, and most children learn quickly to understand their relative meanings. *A* can substitute for a singular *the*, leaving *an* till later; and *some* for the plural *the*. *His* and possessive *her* need a judicious introduction, usually in the object position, but preferably several weeks before or after the object pronouns *him* and *her* are first used, or even the subject pronouns *he* and *she*. Some children find difficulty enough in remembering to use *she* instead of *her* in the subject position, without our adding to it and eliciting, for example, the error *she dog* in place of *her dog*.

Lee groups together the other less frequent determiners, *our, their, these* and *those* with the initiators *some (of the), all (of the), a lot of (the), the other, another,* followed by *both* and *every*. These appear in LARSP Stage VI, which is beyond the immediate goal of the work described in this chapter.

(d) Adjectives. Those which appear the highest in frequency lists are those which can apply to both people and things, or those which describe gross difference, e.g. *big* and *little*. It is useful to be able to use the same selection of adjectives as complements to names, people and things, before using the groups which are applicable mostly to people or mostly to things. Care should be taken to extract uncomplimentary adjectives, e.g. *silly, noisy*, before using the complimentary ones to describe known people with specific names.

2 Gradual removal of clues

Assuming that P has been given and has used all possible clues, and achieves near 100 per cent success, the task is then made more difficult by the gradual elimination of the clues, that is, of noun determiners, parts of the verb *to be*, etc., and the word endings; and all signing, which has been used both by the teacher as a second visual aid to P's memory, and by P as a *kinaesthetic* aid. Some Ps can remember visual images of words which have been removed, and they nod in the direction of each written word and each space as they say each word. The surest way to remove this clue is to ask P to turn his chair round, with his back to the desk. If necessary T can

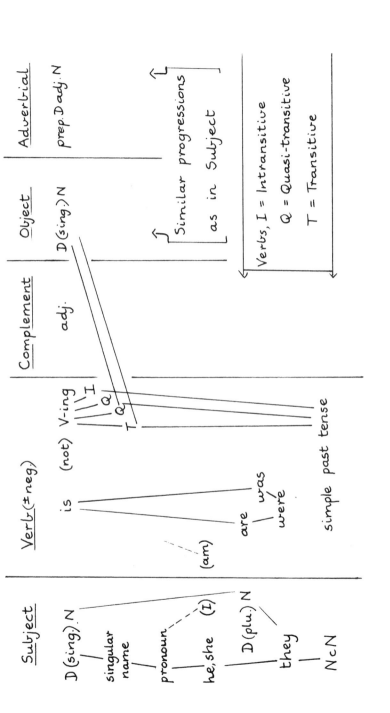

Figure 5.1 Summary of main progressions from Stage II to Stage IV, LARSP

move to face him. This means that no cards at all are visible, and the way is open for T to ask P similarly structured questions about people in pictures, and about people he knows. The memory of the structure of the expected answer is still fresh enough in his mind, so he usually succeeds. Of course the real test of his acquisition of a new structure is whether he uses it in another context, and later with another person, either in answer to a question, or as a spontaneous statement in an unstructured situation.

A structured walk implies the necessity for application of what has been learnt in the classroom. It may be round the school building, or slightly further afield, the only requirement being that people can be seen doing a variety of actions. Most structures can be practised, and Ps soon seem to grasp the notion that this is no ordinary walk. Once each structure can be produced easily in a mobile situation, they can base their remarks on a grammatical structure just as easily as on spontaneous interest. As the response structure has been well practised, it is T who starts asking the stimulus questions. Later in the walk Ps are encouraged to do more questioning. And having talked about happenings in the present continuous tense, the meaning and function of the past continuous can be emphasized by sitting down at the end of the session to remind each other of what was happening, e.g. *What was the man holding?*, *What were the birds eating?* It can be pointed out to any child who argues that the man is probably still holding the bag, or the birds are still eating the bread, that this is an uncertain fact now, but was certain when it was happening, hence the need for the past tense here.

3 The elicitation of questions

When P is familiar with any specific statement structure, he can be encouraged to ask the corresponding question. He has been listening to its model throughout the time he has been answering it. It is wise when changing rôles to change chairs too, so that the questioner is in the position of T, and addresses the questions to the other children and the teacher who has changed places with him. At first P finds questioning much more difficult than he thinks it will be, so T can help him by signing the words for as long as necessary. Not all the Ps in a group are ready for this progression at the same time, which allows the less advanced ones to gain more practice in making statements before it is their turn to become questioners.

Planning a session

It is important to have one aim only per exercise. In each 20-minute session there are a number of ways of ringing the changes, in order to retain the maximum attention. The same goal can be pursued through the whole session, but via different formats. When further practice is needed in a specific item, which the children may have become bored with, the pressure can be removed from it by changing another element in the sequence, e.g. if T's aim is to improve the use of the past tense, she asks P to use a pronoun in the reply, e.g.

S *Did the woman run?*
R *(Yes.) She ran.*

When concentration is required for another element, the original goal is more easily reached. Or, the same grammatical goal can be pursued, and the levels of difficulty, and therefore the amount of challenge, increased by the removal of clues. Two or three different items may be practised. Then they should come from different columns in the analysis, i.e. clause and phrase level combined, and word-endings.

Because visual clues are present, there should be the minimum of errors in the item being practised. If errors are made in another aspect, they can usually be overlooked. If not, the correct version can be spoken casually by the teacher. But if one of the children remarks upon the error, it should be acknowledged but dismissed. There are rare occasions when it should be followed up, especially if it worries the child who made the error. The children's attitude in the session is based on the idea that it is a game which is enjoyable, but which helps to improve their ways of talking. They are usually prepared to change later in the session to an exercise which practises another type of element which they find difficult.

The complete pack of cards

The main pack consists of 300 to 400 cards, representing most of the words in the John Horniman School first-level vocabulary. As there are so many nouns, some have been omitted. Those retained are those which are 'possessable', as these can be used in other syntactic contexts, but the opposite is not true. 'People' nouns can be on cards of a slightly different orange colour from that of 'object' nouns. The three types of personal pronouns (e.g. *I, me, mine*) can be on pink cards of three slightly different tones. This is not always possible, and is not essential. But it gives further visual information about possibilities and limitations in permutations of word-classes. Even when a difference in colour tones is included, there is a minority of children who see no difference at all. This does not matter. We should never expect all children to gain the same degree of information from all clues.

On the cards are:

simple drawings of people, animals or objects:
simple drawings of PGSS signs of verbs, prepositions and adjectives; each word is also written small at the bottom of the card; as described earlier (on page 46), a verb is represented by two cards

stapled together, with the past tense form written at the lower edge of the back card;

large words on the cards which represent all the other closed-class concepts, i.e. noun determiners, pronouns, modals and (other) auxiliaries (including the negative elliptical forms of the most common, e.g. *can't, didn't*) *not, yes* and *no* (several of each).

The reasons for not drawing the PGSS signs for these words is that they are very common, and their written form must be learnt as soon as possible for reading purposes. *Small words* are written at the bottom of the cards representing conjunctions. The reasons for a reduced size of word are that they are introduced much later in the scheme when reading ability probably includes them; and sometimes it is essential that they are chosen and not produced at random. They take up less room when they overlap each other vertically.

The complementary pack consists of all the endings for open-class words, i.e. for verbs (*-ing, -en, -s, -'s, -n't*), for nouns (*-s, -'s, -s'*) and for adjectives (*-est, -er, -ly*). The colour of each word-ending card corresponds to that of the open-class word it follows. Each card is twice the length of the square which is laid on top. This ensures that the child sees the two morphemes as one word. Both verbs and adjectives whose final letter is a single consonant or an *-e*, have the second consonant added feintly, or the final *-e* crossed out feintly. There is no need to point out the reason, but children who ask can be given the explanation, and some of them apply it to their written work in the classroom. The possessive *-'s* should be white, and so should the card for the final apostrophe in the written plural possessive form *-s'*, as in 'the girls' coats'. Their functions correspond to noun-determiners.

The backs of the cards

It is sometimes necessary for T to know something about the word on the card before it is turned over, e.g. when singular and plural subjects are mixed, the question must vary between *Who is . . . ing?* and *Who are . . . ing?* Various hieroglyphics on the back of the cards give this kind of information. A thick dot indicates a singular, and a thick line a plural. If these are put on the same place on each card, e.g. the top left-hand corner, the pack can be re-sorted more quickly, both so that all the cards are facing the same way, and so that they return to their original piles. Noun determiners and pronouns are marked in the same way as nouns. Other information given on the backs of the cards is:

for verbs:	intransitive, quasi-transitive, transitive:
	irregular past, or ending in sound *-t, -d, -id*:
	(e)n past participle or not: whether the questions *where? when?* or *why?* can be asked.
for adjectives:	applicable to people and things, e.g. *big*: not

applicable to people, e.g. *long*: not wise to apply to names, e.g. *silly*: colour

for prepositions: whether they can answer the questions *where?* or *when?* or both.

Storage

Only one person can satisfactorily use each completed set of cards. Specific subsets are combined for a specific group of children, and it is a waste of time to refile all the cards after each session, as the same set is often used for several consecutive sessions. They can conveniently be stored upright in small boxes, the sets being kept together with rubberbands. The following sections have been found to be practicable:

people and animals: singulars; easy plurals, e.g. *girls, boys*; more difficult plurals, e.g. *men, women, a boy and a man*, etc.

pronouns: proper names, subject, object, possessive, e.g. *mine*

auxiliary verbs: *is, am, are, was, were, want to, going to, will*; positive modals; *has to*, etc. *do, does, did, don't, doesn't, didn't*; some negative modals *have, has, had; been*

main verbs: intransitive, e.g. *run, sit*; quasi-transitive, e.g. *eat, draw*; transitive, e.g. *make, push*; ditransitive, e.g. *give, show*; those followed by noun clause objects, e.g. *hope, think*

adjectives: for things *and* people; for things alone; for people alone; numbers

non-human nouns: singular, plural
prepositions
adverbs
not and *n't*
conjunctions: co-ordinating, e.g. *and, but*; subordinating, e.g. *because, if*

noun determiners
yes and *no*

A final section in a box can, for the purposes of time economy and efficiency, contain all sets in current use. (It has proved impossible for remediators to share such a box.)

Use of the cards with other types of children

The card method was designed for use with children with expressive disorders. It is now also being used with the smaller number of children with primarily receptive disorders. They are accustomed to 'reading' the written sentences they compose with either signing and/or spoken words. In the LARSP method they are presented with ready-made sentences, and it helps them to absorb the colour patterns more effectively when they see each one repeatedly in a quick unhindered sequence. When they are working primarily with their own written words, other kinds of activities are interposed, i.e. matching each concept with a written word, remembering the colour pattern, and copying the result.

There is no theoretical reason why a modified form of the card method should not be used with children with other handicaps, e.g. low intelligence, provided that a simple enough type of symbol can be drawn and understood. Bliss symbols are a possible example. Bigger, but fewer cards could be used according to the potential ability of the group.

Effectiveness of this type of remediation

It has not been possible to provide any objective validation. But subjectively it is considered that this method of remediation is more effective than those previously used. We had relied on specific individual and/or group practice given by the speech therapists in their sessions; on different kinds of practice, with an emphasis on written grammar, in the classroom; and on various kinds of corrections given by other adults in the children's environment. These approaches are still used, but probably more as supplements to the spoken, systematically structured one described here. All remediators are working with the same kind of basic information, and in the same broad progression.

During the parts of the programme in which the children are encouraged to complete sentences in their own way, many different grammatical forms are generated. The starter is the sequence of two or three cards in which the same number of concepts are thrown together. This triggers the children's imaginations, and often they produce more than one sentence, or even a complete short story, including rationalizations of any group of concepts which they consider to be inappropriately clustered.

In addition to the improvement in the children's grammar, this method carries with it a number of bonus effects. The ability to read closed-class vocabulary is increased. So is the vocabulary itself. One group, although using the possessives *his* and *her* appropriately, was totally unaware of the existence of the word *their*. They had never 'heard' the word before, but were able to use it correctly after very few examples.

The children gain incidental practice in the use of Paget–Gorman Signed Speech. It is reasonable to suppose that 'kinaesthetic feedback' is at work. The more signing they do, the more the children are able to remember the feel of a grammatical structure in addition to the visual pattern.

The spontaneous writing of some children has become freer and greater in quantity. Reading is another skill which is practised incidentally. The words describing all concepts except the nouns are written on the cards, either alone or in association with the drawing of the sign. This ensures that the spellings of most of the common morphemes, i.e. all the closed-class words and all the word-endings, are read frequently and should become more readily recognizable in other contexts.

The method is freely adaptable. Each remediator devises her own details of technique and progression. Children often produce additional ideas.

The scheme is structured enough to appeal to the children's need for a predictable routine, but flexible enough that it can develop in different ways with groups of children with different needs.

6   *Language Through Reading*

During the early years of the John Horniman School teachers struggled to teach reading with published schemes which were not only incompatible with the natural language of children in normal schools, but which also militated against the consistent, though stilted, grammatical structures being accepted from language disordered children by teachers and speech therapists. Children learned to decode single word by single word, and probably understood the meaning of the text little more than if the words had been presented in lists. This was indeed the format in which test material was presented, the idea then being that we did not want the children to 'guess' the meaning of each word from the so-called textual 'context'! There were no printed books available whose grammatical structures we could expect the children to understand. The individual books we were obliged to make were by no means an ideal response to the problem. But they were better than nothing. Each teacher made wall-charts of reading material, based on the current project, for the whole class to read aloud, both in chorus and as individuals. Gradually each child assumed more responsibility for his own decoding. When the class had become proficient in reading a set of these wall-charts, they were made into a giant book, which was added to the readable material in the book corner.

The need for the use of consistent verb forms had by this time been partially met. We decided to introduce verbs in their present continuous form, as in 'the boy is running'. As each child gradually needed to express the concept of past action, he was taught the past continuous form, as in 'the boy was running'. In this way he had only one change to make in order to express the 'past' concept. When he had grasped this, he was taught how to use the past simple form of verbs. But as there was no accessible model of language development on which to base further decisions, teachers used their intuition when choosing between alternative ways of expressing simple concepts in a written form. The production of individual books is still thought to be a valid method of teaching factual material, and reinforcing the appropriate level of language learning.

Teachers also made books for individual children's needs. Photographs provided by a child's family were a relevant stimulus. The child chose the words, and the teacher the structures. Some parents' weekly letters were so appropriate that they could be assembled within a cover and used as an ideal basis for learning to decode words. But an additional factor was that neither the giant books nor individuals' smaller ones could compete with the attractiveness of the format of printed books.

Language Through Reading: One, Two and Three

One child's struggle with a page of a well-known reading scheme led his teacher to produce yet another type of book. He had struggled not only with the mass of words, but also with the inconsistency of structure. Any available meaning came from the illustration. What we needed was the minimum number of words presented within a common structure, which forced the child into retaining the meaning of the beginning of each sentence while reading the end of it. An immediate test was necessary, and this could be provided by a set of pictures from which the correct one must be chosen. Initially the main aim of the use of books in this format was to teach the early stages of the skill of reading comprehension. Three sentence-subjects and three verbs were chosen. Pictures were searched for in old magazines. And the form of what is now called *Language Through Reading (One)* was born. One child succeeded. Soon the whole class showed its need and appreciation of this kind of simplicity. And about 30 different sets of material were made. The most frequent nouns, verbs, prepositions and adjectives were used, within the simplest clause-structures of Remedial Syntax, for example, 'the girl is walking'. An artist drew the pictures. Eventually the prototype series was succeeded by an even more systematic scheme of 52 sets of material. The first sets correspond not only to the early colour patterns of Remedial Syntax, but also to the stage between LARSP stages II and III, that is, the first, 'blending' of clause-level structures with phrase-level structures. More advanced sets correspond to the next blending stage, between III and IV.

Figure 6.1 Language Through Reading, One: example of two-by-two matrix

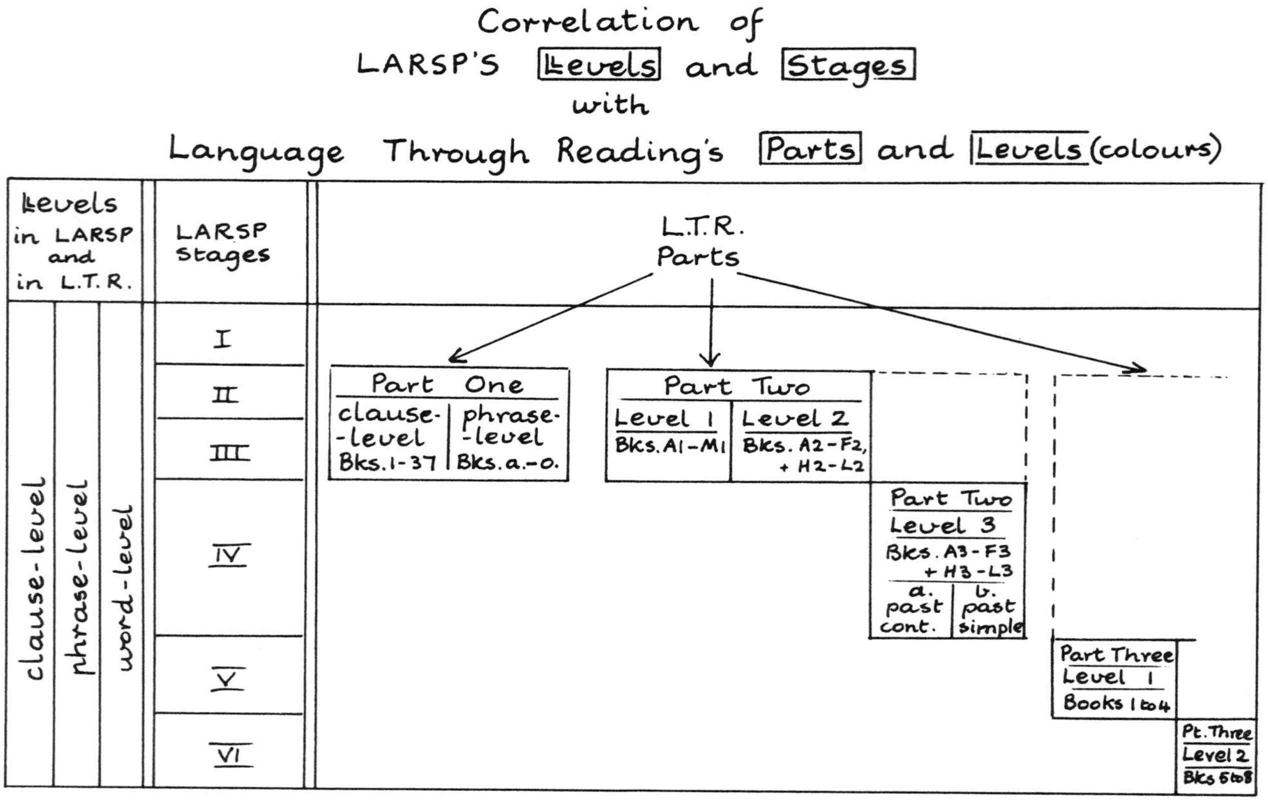

Figure 6.2 Correlation of LARSP's *levels* and *stages* with Language through Reading's *parts* and *levels* (colours)

The other 15 sets of material give the opportunity to practise combinations of meaning within single phrases.

Terms used to describe *Language Through Reading* sets and sub-sets are similar to, but do not entirely correspond with, those used in LARSP. (See Figure 6.2 while reading the remainder of this paragraph.) The accompanying diagram clarifies this. On a LARSP chart, stages are horizontal divisions, and levels are vertical. The 'stages' in Language Through Reading match those in LARSP. So do the 'levels' in Language Through Reading (One). But 'levels' in Language Through Reading (Two) and Language Through Reading (Three) are horizontal subdivisions. Books A 1 to M 1 at Level 1 of Language Through Reading (Two) use similar grammatical constructions to those in Language Through Reading (One). Books A 2 to F 2 and H 2 to L 2, include pronouns, plurals, 'not', 'very', and 'and', but are still synthesized according to LARSP's stages II and III. Language Through Reading (Two) Level 3 matches LARSP stage IV. All '3 a' books contain past continuous verb-forms, and all '3 b' books contain appropriate past simple forms. Language Through Reading (Three), Level 1, corresponds to LARSP's stage V, and Language Through Reading (Three), Level 2, to LARSP's stage VI.

Language Through Reading (One)

The scheme is now published. Its primary purpose has changed. It now aims to teach the early stages of language, in a written and printed form. 'Remedial Syntax' gives practice in composing sentences to match a given situation or drawing. But a Language Through Reading booklet requires a child to decode the marks on the paper, and to prove his understanding of them by the choice of the appropriate picture. The task is still matching, but the stimulus and response are reversed.

And the transition is taught by a series of intermediate matching tasks, using the additional material, comprising words, phrases, and simple sentences which correspond to the same set of pictures which test comprehension of the text in the booklet.

But first the pictures themselves must be 'understood'. To this end they are sorted, first according to one set of criteria, for example, the subjects; and next, according to another set, for example, the verbs. There are three separate babies, three separate men, and three separate women; each of these people is eating, or drinking, or walking. After a little practice with the first sets, a child soon learns that a grid can be made with the drawings. Then the drawings can be labelled with the appropriate noun-phrase strips placed on the left of each row, and with the appropriate verb-phrase strips placed above each column. Variations in clause-type suggest that the phrase labels may be put at the bottom of the column and on the right of each row, as in the set, 'holding the apple, eating the cake, cutting the egg'.

Either before this task, or by means of it, a child realizes that the words on the strips refer, for example, to 'the baby', whatever he is doing; and, for example, to 'is drinking', whoever is the subject. Until this level of generalization has been grasped, no further progress can be made.

Then, the drawings are presented singly, and the child selects the correct noun-phrase of the three possibilities given him; the process is repeated with the verb-phrases. The process of true reading, that is, the decoding of marks on paper, is approached by reversing the task. This time the child is shown noun-phrases or verb-phrases singly; he must find all three drawings which each one describes: the process is repeated with the other type of phrase.

This is followed by a more complex matching task. Given one drawing at a time, can the child find both phrases which describe it? The stimulus is still the drawing, and the phrases are still the response. The process can be reversed, still using the phrase-strips.

The last matching-task before the booklet is read is to find the complete-sentence strip which describes each drawing. This too can be reversed, the teacher presenting each sentence strip and asking for the matching drawing. The child's thinking behind this last task is identical to that which he uses for the booklet. As each sentence in the booklet is read and understood, the appropriate drawing is found and placed on the opposite page. Although each page in the original booklets contained a slot into which a drawing was placed, the thinking process demanded by the revised 'transparent' pocket-format is identical.

The assembled booklet is checked by the teacher, who can return it if she finds the pictures incorrectly matched. The final task, or any of the preceding ones, can be repeated until drawing-to-sentence matches are 100 per cent correct.

The choice of vocabulary was based firstly on the criterion of very high frequency of open-class words among normal children of five and six years old; and secondly on the optimum possibilities of noun/verb and noun/adjective pairs, and noun/verb/noun trios. The inclusion of as many as 19 different verbs, and the small number of nouns, within a total vocabulary-load of less than 100 words, reflects the importance of the introduction of appropriate verbs alongside the subject- and object-nouns whose meanings are the easiest to grasp. The sooner the child can learn to use verbs meaningfully, the sooner he learns to construct simple sentences. A minimum number of closed-class words is included, as it is essential to repeat them so that their use is shown to be necessary, and becomes automatic. The most efficient way to teach Language Through Reading vocabulary is by any whole-word method. Phonic analysis is not appropriate at this early stage of sentence construction.

Although many of the concept-grids are three-by-three, as described, the earliest are two-by-two, so that the technique is introduced in as simple a way as possible. This number is more satisfactory than an array which proved to be more difficult, that is, one-by-four. A subject doing four different verbs, or a verb being done by four different subjects is only one row or one column, and therefore not a grid; and the memory-load of four verbs or four nouns appeared to be much greater than that of two verbs and two nouns.

Teachers ask questions of the children throughout all the processes, as naturally as they do in any other teaching situation. The reason for asking questions here is to teach the meaning of the question forms 'who?', 'what?', 'what . . . doing?', 'what . . . [verb]-ing?' and 'where?'. The specific accuracy of the answer given by the child is not so vital as is some indication that he has understood the question. To the question, about the drawing of a man eating a cake, 'who is eating?' the reply 'the boy' is more acceptable, although inaccurate, than 'the cake'; and for 'what is the man eating?', 'the egg' is more acceptable than 'the man', or 'eating'; all of which, in actual verbal transactions, have been given.

All of the materials can also be used for other purposes, such as handwriting models, spelling practice, stimuli for simple drawings or sentences; and further reinforcement of the meaning of single words, phrases and sentences is given by manual signing. Children can work in pairs, which expands the conversation. For more able children the drawings serve as stimuli for writing or speaking more advanced sentence structures, using, for example, pronouns, modal verbs, or noun-clause objects.

Language Through Reading (One) has also been used as a basis for an experimental initial reading method. Children learn to read coloured shapes of words before any letters are introduced. The method was found to be successful with a child with whom every previous attempt had resulted in failure. (See page 68). Other children are learning by it and enjoying it.

Language Through Reading (Two)

Language Through Reading (Two) can be said to comprise within itself a grid of booklets. (See figure 6.3.) Each row, represented by a colour and a number, includes a group of grammatical items within 'Remedial Syntax' and 'LARSP', which is now dovetailed into a suggested 'Grammatical Sequence'. (See Chapters 2 and 5.)

In each column of books, represented by a letter, a similar story is repeated, most of the variations being based on the increasing difficulty of grammatical structure. The vocabulary of Language Through Reading (One) is repeated in the first six books. There is only one additional word, 'school'. Because the vocabulary is so familiar, the child's attention is drawn to the meaning of each sentence, and the relationships between the sentences on each page and between the pages in each book. There are visible meaning sequences down each page and through each book. The line-drawings are used, not to test, as in Language Through Reading (One), but to illustrate, that is, to clarify the meaning of the sentences, and

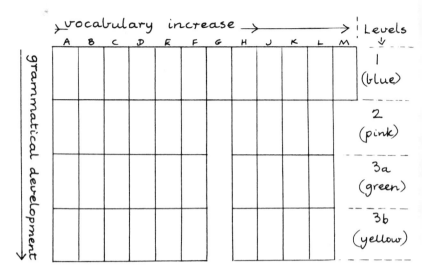

Figure 6.3   Language Through Reading, Two: grid to show the relationship between the 52 booklets

to check that they have been understood correctly.

Some children need the reinforcement of colour to which they have become accustomed in 'Remedial Syntax' work. So teachers underline each word in the early books. The concept of word-class is further emphasized by the class-grouping of words in lists at the back of the books. The proportion of verbs is even higher than in Language Through Reading (One).

Having been introduced to the concept of a real book through familiar vocabulary, the child progresses to read the next six books at the same grammatical level, but with open-class vocabulary new to him. The two letters G and M refer to books at this level only. The versatile noun 'box' serves to increase verb-vocabulary; likewise the useful verb 'washing' is used with many different nouns.

In both the first and second levels of Language Through Reading (Two), the present continuous form of the verb is used. This complements its initial use both in 'Remedial Syntax' and in Language Through Reading (One). The differences between the first two levels seem at first sight minimal, but teach the comprehension of some very important additional structures, that is, regular noun plurals, introduced first of all as the objects of sentences, in which the final –s is the only difference between the plural and singular forms. When plurals later appear in the subject phrase, they must be followed by the changed auxiliary 'are'. Pronouns replace some nouns; 'and' connects two nouns, or names; the negative 'not' and the intensifier 'very' are included in the text. These eight closed-class words make far more difference to the meaning than their number would imply.

There are more differences in the third level. In order to increase interest, and to introduce past tenses, some details in the stories are changed. And some irregular nouns appear, some new noun-determiners and adjectival phrases; and some common one-word adverbs. At the same level, the past continuous tense is introduced. So substantially the same stories are told, but they are not happening now: they *were* happening. As in the grammatical sequence, on which the progression through the rows is based, the past continuous form is used to introduce the representation of the concept of 'past'. Once this concept has been grasped, the change in form can be tolerated. This follows the principle that, wherever possible, only one unfamiliar linguistic concept should be taught at a time. More than one is confusing.

So the other version of Level 3 of Language Through Reading (Two) includes, wherever it is appropriate, the simple past forms of verbs. (See figure 6.4.2: levels 3a and 3b.) Some of the past continuous forms must, however, be retained. Both forms are necessary in normal usage, and can now be accepted by the children, and gradually the subtle difference between them is being absorbed.

Throughout Language Through Reading (Two) closed-class vocabulary increases to about 60 words; and open-class vocabulary principally through the inclusion of past tenses, increases to over 200 words.

An essential part of the Language Through Reading (Two) set of materials is the question-cards. There is one to accompany every page of text. Children work more independently than with Language Through Reading (One), and usually the answers to the questions are written. But their separation from the book enables them to be used flexibly: covering the illustration; covering the text; alongside both; or alone, with the book out of sight. The answers to the questions can be deduced by re-reading the text. At first the questions match the text. There may be two questions for one line of text, but they are in the same sequence as the text. Later, they do not match, and the search for the answer is more difficult, especially for those children who try to do this task without considering meaning. The lack of alignment forces such children to think more conceptually. If the question card is covering the text, children must not only think of the appropriate answer to each question, but also know how to spell the necessary words. If the book is not to hand, a longer-term memory is necessary. But only a few children are as advanced as this. With some children the teacher asks the questions orally, and requires spoken or signed answers before they are written down. Some children can work through this process on their own, signing each question to themselves, or reading it aloud, and giving themselves the answer in the same way. Some have found it beneficial, or even necessary, to themselves, to encode the original text into signing. This provides a definite link between reading and understanding, and therefore increases enjoyment.

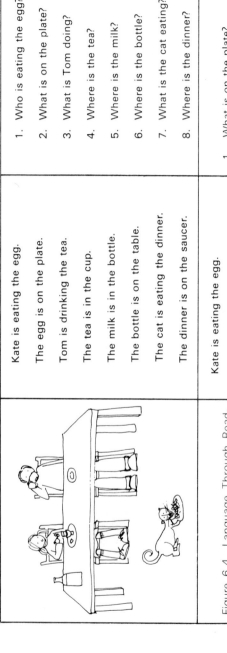

Kate is eating the egg.	1. Who is eating the egg?
The egg is on the plate.	2. What is on the plate?
Tom is drinking the tea.	3. What is Tom doing?
The tea is in the cup.	4. Where is the tea?
The milk is in the bottle.	5. Where is the milk?
The bottle is on the table.	6. Where is the bottle?
The cat is eating the dinner.	7. What is the cat eating?
The dinner is on the saucer.	8. Where is the dinner?

Kate is eating the egg.	1. What is on the plate?
It is on the plate.	2. What is Kate doing?
Tom is drinking the tea.	3. What is in the cup?
It is in the cup.	4. What is in the bottle?
The milk is in the bottle.	5. What is Tom doing?
The bottle is on the table.	6. Where is the bottle?
The cat is eating the dinner.	7. Whose dinner is on the saucer?
The cat's dinner is on the saucer.	

Figure 6.4 Language Through Reading, Two: examples of drawing, text and questions showing differences between each one, and more advanced vocabulary and grammar.
A. Note some of the more advanced structures in Level Two: 1 Pronouns; 2 Possessive -'s. On other pages are: 3 Plural objects, e.g. plates; 4 names connected with 'and', e.g. Kate and Tom, followed by 'are . . . -ing. 5 not; 6 very. And questions are not aligned.

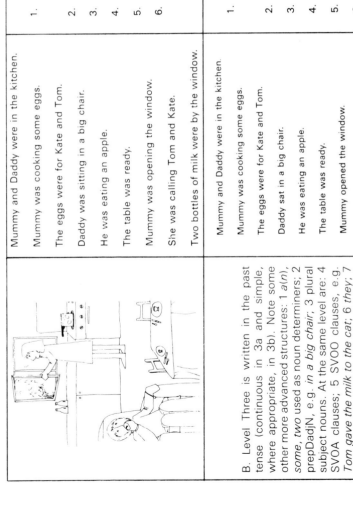

B. Level Three is written in the past tense (continuous in 3a and simple, where appropriate, in 3b). Note some other more advanced structures: 1 *a(n)*, *some*, *two* used as noun determiners; 2 prepDadjN, e.g. *in a big chair*; 3 plural subject nouns. At the same level are: 4 SVOA clauses; 5 SVOO clauses, e.g. *Tom gave the milk to the cat*; 6 *they*; 7 adverbs, e.g. *quietly*, *again*.

Mummy and Daddy were in the kitchen.

Mummy was cooking some eggs.

The eggs were for Kate and Tom.

Daddy was sitting in a big chair.

He was eating an apple.

The table was ready.

Mummy was opening the window.

She was calling Tom and Kate.

Two bottles of milk were by the window.

1. Were Mummy and Daddy in the house?

2. Were Tom and Kate in the house?

3. What was Mummy cooking?

4. What was Daddy eating?

5. Where was Daddy sitting?

6. How many bottles of milk were by the window?

Mummy and Daddy were in the kitchen.

Mummy was cooking some eggs.

The eggs were for Kate and Tom.

Daddy sat in a big chair.

He was eating an apple.

The table was ready.

Mummy opened the window.

She called Tom and Kate.

Two bottles of milk were by the window.

1. Were Mummy and Daddy in the house?

2. Were Tom and Kate in the house?

3. What was Mummy cooking?

4. What was Daddy eating?

5. Was the table ready?

6. How many bottles of milk were by the window?

The order of question forms is developmental according to the research of Tyack (1974) and Hart, Walker and Gray (1975). Some teachers underline the question-words on the question-cards with the colour of the required response, as an aid to sentence analysis. Although children with severe receptive disorders may find it easier to start by giving whole-sentence responses, they are all encouraged to select the correct phrase-response only. This practice ensures that they understand the question-word. For example, for a simple sentence in the text structured subject + verb + object, three different questions can be asked.

'Who is [verb]-ing [the object]?'
'What is [the subject] doing?'
'What is [the subject] [verb]-ing?'

Phrase answers, respectively, are

'The subject. . . .'
' . . . [verb]-ing [the object].'
' . . . [the object].'

Conversely, the complete sentence answers all three questions and, with this, question-comprehension would not be checked.

At Level 3 the scope of questions is extended, to require simple inferences. At first these are simplified by the use of forced alternatives, for example, 'Was Tom in the kitchen or in the bedroom?' Sometimes a question refers to a statement made earlier in the text, or to information supplied only by the drawing opposite the text. This helps the children to understand simple relationships between the pages of the story, and its underlying sequence.

The past simple version of Level 3 also includes work-cards, in order to introduce this new format to a child while he is still familiar with the content and structural level of their referents.

The set of 52 booklets can be used flexibly. It is not necessary for every child to work through all of them. A child who is not discouraged by the sight of unfamiliar vocabulary and new structures simultaneously can omit H J K L of Level 1 and A B C D E F of Level 2. If in his spontaneous speech he is using both forms of the past tense appropriately, he probably does not need to read the first version of Level 3. But a child who needs to read every book does not get bored with the repetition of stories. He learns slowly enough that he may not remember the story well, or he may be pleased to be reminded of a familiar one.

Language Through Reading (Three)

Language Through Reading (One) teaches the concept of the meaning of written symbols; ways of combining meanings; and comprehension of the resulting simple sentences. Language Through Reading (Two) extends vocabulary-recognition and grammatical structure; with it, children's ability to understand and use basic language is reinforced. But it became obvious that a final link must be provided between a very systematic presentation and the more natural language of more advanced books which the children would want to read, some of which is included in LARSP Stages V and VI. Language Through Reading (Three) was devised to meet this need.

It comprises eight books, of varying length, but still as short as the individual stories in longer books. Most of the vocabulary is still within the basic list. The stories grew from grouping unused nouns together, and combining them imaginatively. This resulted in a variety of styles. The structured basis is still the Grammatical Sequence, the combination of Remedial Syntax with LARSP stages. The first four books (known as Level 1) include V structures, and the other four, (Level 2), Stage VI structures. Other main differences between these books and those in Language Through Reading (Two) relate to the drawings, the meanings of closed-class words, and the question forms.

Drawings are more detailed. They appear at irregular intervals, and not necessarily at the same spread as the relevant part of the text. In some instances they provide more information than the text, encouraging children to scrutinize them carefully, especially when they are searching for the answers to some of the questions. Conversely, some parts of the action are deliberately not illustrated at all.

At first the stories were written very simply. But it was considered essential at this stage to introduce as many as possible of the closed-class words which had so far been avoided. They must be encountered here if a practical link were to be made with more advanced reading material. They are, after all, the most common words in use. Without them the nouns, verbs and adjectives themselves would convey only impoverished ideas. Language disordered children have great difficulty in making generalizations, especially those involving abstractions as difficult as those expressed in quantity- space- and time- vocabulary. So the basic closed-class words were packed into the story shells, resulting in richer, more interesting, subtler language. The children appreciated this, and some were soon able to tolerate the greater demands made on their thinking processes.

Extensions in meaning includes concepts of time, manner, and causality. To test these ideas 'when?', 'how?' and 'why?' are frequent question-words. But the children's comprehension of the concepts represented by the closed-class vocabulary needed to be tested. In order to heighten teachers' awareness of specific comprehension difficulties in this area, simple drawings on cards are provided, illustrating some aspects of the meanings of these words. These accompany each book, and are used as talking points between teacher and child before the book is begun. The teacher thus ensures that the child has an adequate under-standing of these essential words in speech, or at least in sign, before they surprise him among known words in the text.

Questions which follow the reading of the text are related to more linguistic expansion, for example, the recursion of LARSP, Stage VI. The intention is to encourage the use of this kind of connective in the children's free written work.

Reading

Although the primary aim of the whole scheme 'Language Through Reading' is to teach language, it has the bonus effect of teaching reading too. Children who begin by knowing nothing of either, learn language and reading together. Those whose spoken grammatical ability is greater than their reading skill may be using the scheme primarily to learn reading. Whatever is known better, assists the child to learn the other, or both skills progress together.

Without a scheme like Language Through Reading, which solves potential problems in learning to read before they are encountered, it is very difficult to teach the skill to language disordered children. The written structures in most reading schemes not only militate against the learning of reading, but consequently provide language patterns which are quite unsuitable in this context, because they are either too advanced, or unfamiliar, or both. But for teachers who are forced by lack of resources into this unequal and unprofitable struggle, it is necessary to outline the type of problems which may have to be overcome in some other way.

An example is drawn from a tape-recorded reading sample by an eight-year-old boy with a severe problem in expressive language, and a comparable one in learning to read. He was intelligent and highly-motivated. Several successive teachers used a variety of methods, and eventually he achieved partial success by learning to 'read' more than 90 coloured word-shapes which gradually incorporated written words. Content was based on John's experience. Figure 6.5 gives a brief indication of a few of John's words, and of the progression from coloured shapes drawn on squared paper to conventional typed words. The colours corresponded to those in Remedial Syntax. Even when John could read his 90 typed words with no errors, his difficulties with printed words still persisted, but to a lesser degree than previously. The text in Table 6.1 is taken from 'Racing to Read' Book Two, page 7. John chose the book himself. He had previously managed to read most of Book One, which included the words 'chimney', 'roof', 'door', 'red', and 'blue'. He could see no difference between a chimney and a roof, so these he read interchangeably. The words 'roof' and 'door' looked the same, as to John the only difference was that between the initial 'd-' and the final '-f'. 'Door' and 'red' were very similar. And, because of his colour-naming confusion, so were 'red' and 'blue'. His attempt to read the four lines was recorded when his enthusiasm was at its height. Two additional words

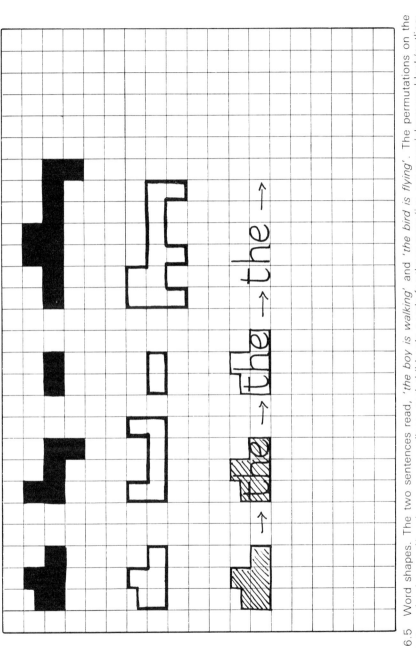

Figure 6.5 Word shapes. The two sentences read, 'the boy is walking' and 'the bird is flying'. The permutations on the presentation of colour and/or shape seem endless, and children's needs for these vary (i.e. presence/absence; block/outline; large/small; handwriting/typing/printing).

Table 6.1: *Transcript of John's tape-recorded reading sample.*
Each numbered sentence is copied from the book. John repeated his attempts either when he thought he was wrong or when it was suggested he should try again.

1	The roof	and	chimney	of	my	doll's	house	are	red
	The blue	and							
	The window	and	the						
	The door	and	the window	of	mine	Brenda's	house	are	red
	The door	and							
	The chimney	and	the roof						
	The chimney	and	and chimney	of	mine	doll's	house	is	red
2	The door	of	Brenda's	house	is	blue			
	The chimney	of	Brenda's	house	is	red			
						blue			
						window			
						chimney			
	The roof								
	The blue								
	The door	of	Brenda's	house	is	blue			
3	The	windows	of	my	doll's	house	are	big	
	The	Brendas	of	mine	house				
					doll is	house	was	big	
	The	windows	of	mine	Brenda's	house	is	blue	
	The	window	of	my	Brenda's	house	are	big	
4	Brenda	is	by	the	door	of	the	doll's	house
	Brenda	is	by	the	window				
					door	of	the	Brenda's	house

were 'Brenda', auditorily associated with 'window', and 'doll', too easily associated with the word 'Brenda', the name of the doll. John knew he would have difficulty, but was more than willing to do his best.

Many language disordered children share some of John's problems, but most do not have all of them. Perhaps he would have found reading hard even if he had had no difficulty in spoken language. This probably exacerbated the problem.

Dear Mr. Greenfild, thank you for frou
cake. we eat the cake on worday and
for eat. I am in beb otbay. it si sun.
the cake was vrey doog and
I had ot eat it witham had.
It is the Chissam benberd otday
and I am riring the letters in
bob. I am Jim who is rering
the letters. I rish you here
the a happy Chssiaber.
                love farm Jim.

Figure 6.6   Transcription of Jim's letter

Jim was one of the children with associated difficulties in spelling. (See figure 6.6) His attempt 'benberd', which was intended to be 'dinner', reflected exactly a similar misperception in reading. Jack could not get started. But his mother's weekly letters were an ideal basis for a language-experience approach, which proved slow, but successful. John, Jim and Jack all found eventually that the phonic associations they learned, laboriously, though spelling, were useful in reading, but not until they had first gained a very firm foundation of 100 or 200 words via a whole-word method.

Joe very quickly learnt the skill of decoding print into spoken words. But they held no meaning for him. When asked a simple question about the text, he mentally turned the pages of the book, selected one, repeated a sentence which bore some resemblance to the question, and 'read' what his long-term memory had stored.

If a scheme like Language Through Reading had been available, these four children would undoubtedly have benefited from using it.

The functional reading ages of all the children are well below that of their peers. They learn slowly, but now far more surely than their predecessors.

7   Spelling: A two-pronged approach

One of the main hindrances to learning in a child with a severe specific language disorder is his poor auditory skill. One of the main tasks of his teachers is to remedy this. Because he has difficulty in understanding the language he hears, he has to learn through the two visual media of signing and reading. One of the approaches to reading is through copying sentences describing known situations which have been composed with a string of words written on small card slips. This is described in Chapter 2. One of the reasons for the success of this technique is that it uses the teaching principle of leading from the known to the unknown. In this context, a familiar situation is the known element, and the marks on paper are the unknown. The child's motivation comes from his interest in the known. The same is true of spelling in general. Once a child becomes really interested in learning to write his own name from memory, it is easy to teach him to do so. A model is provided, which he copies repeatedly until he can dispense with it. Immediately he is encouraged to write the names of other people, and things. These can soon be included in simple sentences. The language-experience approach to reading has begun.

Whole-word spelling

Some children who use Remedial Syntax become proficient spellers automatically. All the words which are added to their folders are meaningful. They use them in so many sentences and copy them so many times, that they become able to write each complete word without noting its individual letters.

The children who learn more slowly can be given the additional help of the technique of finger-tracing. This was described in 1943 by Grace Fernald in *Remedial Techniques in Basic School Subjects*. She called it the visual-auditory-kinaesthetic-tactile (VAKT) approach. It bridges the gap between the visual and auditory modalities, which is often a very difficult connection to make, and it has proved its value consistently during many years of use.

The teacher shows a written word to a pupil in close association with the object, model or picture, or, if the pupil really understands the spoken word, in association with this alone.

The word is written in bold felt-marker script on a piece of sugar paper about 20×7 cm. Each slip of paper should be colour-coded. (See Chapter 2.) The child traces the word with his forefinger. As he traces, he

Plate 7.1   Together with a visual reminder of its meaning the word is being finger traced and spoken.

continually repeats the whole word, without matching each sound and letter phonically. When he feels competent to do so he attempts to write the word with his forefinger in a sand tray, so that he can see the finished word, or on a smooth surface. When he achieves the correct version, returning to the original word for further practice if necessary, he writes the word on paper or a blackboard. This method is the most effective if words are finger-traced as if the letters are joined. So the letters must be presented so that the spaces between them can be filled with an obvious join.

A child is likely to remember the spelling for future use because he has first learnt it as a whole word. The intermediate steps he takes when tracing the word letter by letter with his finger or a pencil should be discarded as soon as possible. He cannot be said to know the spelling until he has written the word unaided without first seeing it. Instead of finger-tracing, a child may copy the required word from a paper or the blackboard. But this is usually found to be less effective, as the tactile element has been removed. This has proved to be more important than the auditory element for children with severe language disorders.

There are certain children, certain words and certain stages in learning to spell, with which a whole-word method is even more necessary, because of learning disorders in the children, or irregularities in the words, or both.

Children with receptive language disorders are those who have the greatest difficulty with learning phonic associations, and who therefore learn more spellings kinaesthetically than phonically. So do the children with problems in sequencing tasks and poor auditory memory. But the children who later prove successful with phonic methods still need to learn their first spellings by finger-tracing. As they begin to understand phonic associations, the more primitive whole-word method can be discarded for words whose phonic rules they have learned, but retained for words with less frequent spelling patterns. Many common words fall into this category. Some children need to be given a brief explanation of the reason for these two methods of learning to spell. Some of them can understand that, the more spelling they learn, by either method, the easier they will find it to distinguish between the two types.

The first words learned by a finger-tracing method are selected according to the criterion of each child's spontaneous speech or signing vocabulary. If this consists mainly of nouns, these are the spellings to be presented first. But for a child who uses words which are syntactically more advanced, such as 'was' or 'they', these words can be included. 'Was' is not only one of the most common words in use; it is also one of the most irregular. It not only begins with a semivowel, which could be written, phonically decoded, just as well by 'oo' as by 'w'; but also includes a medial vowel which 'sounds' as if it should be written with an 'o'; and a final consonant which could be written with a 'z'. Even more urgent exceptions to primary phonic rules are 'the' and 'is'. Other such words are 'were', 'four', 'fire', and 'learn'. There are not enough examples of really frequent words which could be added to any of these, to form teachable word-groups. Most closed-class words are in this category.

In order to meet specific needs of individual children, teachers use whole-word lists which have been designed for adaptation to a variety of needs. They are presented in a three-fold classification: first according to broad word-classes, that is, verbs, nouns, adjectives, and all the closed-class words together; secondly, according to word-length; and thirdly, the order within the lists is based on frequency, in the same way as the whole of the basic vocabulary.

It is wise to provide in every classroom a box full of words, probably a few hundred. They are arranged in 26 groups, according to initial letters. Some teachers prefer to arrange the words in strict dictionary order. This can best be attained if a rule can be kept about replacing each borrowed word with a name-card of the borrower. This ensures that a child takes only one word at a time, and reduces the necessity for the teacher to restore order in the box at the end of every school day.

A child who needs to rely heavily on the finger-tracing method has his own set of words, either a few in a big envelope, or many in a small box. He asks for words to be added more often than the other children, but enjoys discarding the copies of the words he finally learns to spell from memory.

In some classrooms every child is assigned a small group of those

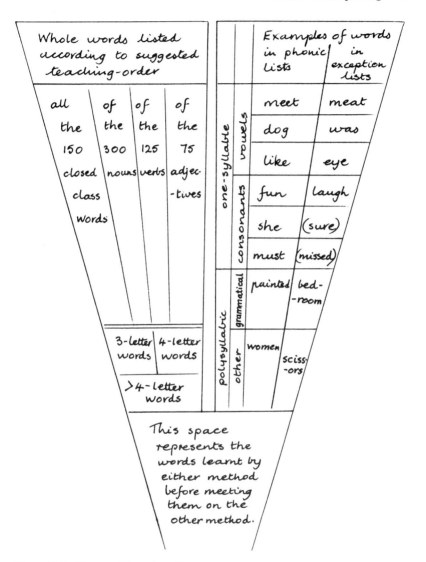

Figure 7.1   The teaching of spelling: a two-pronged approach

relevant to him, to be learned within a week during odd moments. Each child proves he can spell each word by writing it on a partitioned area of the blackboard. This activity is highly motivating, as it produces visible results, and also appeals to the desire of language disordered children for a predictable learning routine.

The finger-tracing method is flexible enough that any words needed in 'spontaneous' written work, such as letter-writing, can be learned in the same way, and incorporated for future use into whatever system is used in the classroom.

Phonics

Most children with severe disorders of the understanding and use of spoken language find that the process of learning to read unfamiliar material is very slow. Although their ability to decode visually is not usually as poor as their auditory skill, they do not learn as fast as their normal peers. Sometimes a teacher tries to help a child by pointing out common phonic associations, but this rarely succeeds, because too many steps are required in the decoding process. One of these steps is phonic spelling. This is a more accessible goal, and it eventually also leads to the improvement of some phonic ability in the reading process.

Phonic reading

A phonic attack on an unfamiliar word which has to be read presupposes certain basic knowledge in the reader: that there is in most words a one-to-one relationship between a sound, or a sound group as in '-x-', and a letter, or a letter group as in '-sh-', and that there is a sequential correspondence between sounds in a spoken word perceived and executed temporally, and the letters in a written word perceived and executed spatially. The reader must know which sounds correspond to which letters and be able to decode the letters into sounds, either physically or mentally; he has to remember the sequence of these sounds, and then blend them into a word he recognizes. A teacher normally expects a reader to repeat these processes several times, and then to understand the total meaning of the words thus decoded. Even more than this, she expects the reader to comprehend the total meaning of a sequence of sentences, and of a series of pages in a book, but this sequence of processes proves too difficult for most language-disordered children. Instead the complementary sequence is taught.

Phonic spelling

A phonic attack on an unfamiliar word which has to be spelled in a written form is simpler. The basic knowledge about phonic associations and sequencing is the same. The writer must learn the letters which most commonly represent all the sounds. When he hears a word, either spoken by someone else, or said physically or mentally by him, he must write the letters in the same order in which he has heard the sounds. And when he has written his version of the word, it is there for him to look at. This is probably the reason why the phonic process in spelling is less daunting than the reverse process in reading. The speller has made his own visual aid. He may alter what he has written, until he is satisfied that it conforms to what he heard. Errors are possible at any step in the process, but the phonic writer has more opportunity to revise his opinion than the phonic reader. On the other hand, he has no contextual clues. But he has written what the teacher hopes he will continue to recognize as the word he was attempting to write.

Practising this skill, for a language-disordered child, must be systematic. A number of regular phonic associations must be taught in order to prove the concept that at least some consistencies exist. Although the thinking behind such a scheme cannot be linear, the scheme itself should be presented in a linear fashion. An earlier scheme, which provided choices for the teacher throughout, proved to be too difficult in practice to transmit. The principles behind the present scheme are the same, but its revised version is more comprehensible, and immediately usable.

Content of a systematic scheme

The phonic programme comprises all the words, more than 700, in the basic 'John Horniman Vocabulary (revised 1982)'. In addition are all the variations on these words, such as :

    plural forms of nouns
    past tenses of verbs
    comparatives of adjectives
    elisions, e.g. can't, let's, etc.

This brings the total number of spellings to more than 1,000.

The grouping of the words

The progression is spiral in nature. One-syllable words are learnt first, then two-syllable, and finally those with three syllables or more. Within all of these categories the phonically regular words are learnt first. 'Irregular' spellings are, however, not excluded from the scheme: several short lists of words are grouped together; and single exceptions are presented after these, that is, words like 'eye', 'sew', and 'you', whose vowel-spellings are so irregular that they are different from all the other words in this limited vocabulary. The latter are among those which must of course be learnt by a whole-word method. They are included within the phonic scheme for the sake of completeness. Many of them are frequent closed-class words. Although they are inserted between the phonically-regular lists, they can be learned or revised at any time, preferably soon after they are introduced within the grammatical sequence of Remedial Syntax. Some of the longer closed-class words are more groupable, and some are included in the open-class lists. But those which are not mixed with the nouns, verbs and adjectives could constitute a separate part of the spelling programme. The words in some word-classes, for example, plural possessive determiners and pronouns (our, your, their; ours, yours, theirs) are presented together despite their phonic dissimilarity because of their semantic and visual similarity. Throughout the programme small groups of words which are often confused with each other are inserted. Some of these are the four-letter words with an initial 'w . . .; (want, what, went, when, were, etc.), and words with a difficult '-l-' in the sound or spelling (for example; pool, pull, field, help).

Some words appear in more than one list. This ensures that, even if the lists are presented in an order deviating from the numbered one, all

Table 7.1: *Phonic progression through vowels and consonants*
Vowels

2 letters 1 sound	1 letter 1 sound	2 letters 2 sounds	some secondary spellings	further differ- ences	poly- syllabic words
short oo, and long vowels -oo, -ee- -ar-, -ir- or	short vowels i, a, e, o, u	diphthongs -i-e -a-e -ou- -o-e -air	all vowel sounds	further spellings of vowel sounds	

Consonants

1 letter 1 sound	2 letters 1 sound	2 letters 2 sounds			
single conso- nants (except x)	-sh -th(e) -th(ing) -ng -ll -ck	-sp- -nt- and other consonant blends		Secondary spellings of consonants including plurals & other morphemes	

examples at that level are included, e.g., black is in the *bl*. . . . list, and also in the. . . . *ck* list.

The names of the children themselves, and of the adults known to them all, are incorporated by each teacher into appropriate learning groups. So are the names of places, roads and other proper nouns when necessary.

Learning phonic associations
Much of a speech therapist's work with a child with a severe language disorder is concerned with a child's sound system. She may use written or printed letters as visual reminders of the sounds she would like him to produce. In doing this she is simultaneously teaching him the early stages of learning the significance of phonic associations. In the classroom the stimulus and response are reversed: the teacher says a sound, and the child either finds the letter it represents, from a small selection before him, or tries to write it. Before the word-scheme is embarked upon, children must be able to distinguish between single-consonant sound–letter correspondences. There are a number of ways in which classroom teaching and practice can be presented. It is important to teach the constancy of the one-to-one relationship in the primary association of sounds and letters. The following is a suggested order for teaching the first 17 single consonants.This order is based on a consideration of all the visual and auditory factors which limit confusion in establishing the necessary associations. The first 11 consonants should be learnt before any attempt is made to combine them with vowels.

   c m d v p s n b f g t   (h l w y r j are left till later)

In early handwriting lessons children learn to copy these letters legibly, recognizing and attempting to reproduce the appropriate differences between them. The teacher points out the phonic qualities of words which contain primary phonic associations. These are the sounds which represent the 17 consonants most frequent in common single-syllable words (i.e. all except k, q, x and z). The teacher does not emphasize deviations from these. So the children associate written letters with their primary sounds and lip-read patterns. When they hear or see a spoken sound, they can write its corresponding letter. For spelling purposes it is not necessary at this stage for children to say the sound when they see the letter. But it helps the learning process, making use of the feedback for reinforcement if they can do it. Also it is the first stage of phonic reading. Or, if a child is totally incapable of learning the sounds of consonants as he learns to write them he is provided with the visual aid of a consonant-chart, or only part of it. He also has a set of the same letters, on separate cards. During the teaching of primary phonic associations of consonants, the teacher says a single sound. The child selects the card representing that sound and covers the identical one on the chart. Gradually the whole chart is covered.

Memory is trained, both for two sounds and for the sequence of these

Table 7.2: *A consonant matrix*

p	t				c/k
b	d				g
f	th(in)	s	sh	ch	h
v	th(e)	z	(gara)ge**	j	
m	n				ng
w		r	l		y

** included here for completeness, but usually omitted.

sounds. Different kinds of pairs can be presented, but all should be taken from words that appear in the basic vocabulary list. At this stage there is no spare time to waste on words which lie beyond it.

A number of stages are suggested in the presentation of two or more sounds.

The teacher says:-

1   The first sound which the child writes; and then the second which the child also writes.
2   The pair several times, emphasizing or elongating each phoneme in turn, until the child has written the pair in the correct order, for example, ar—/m—, or c—/ar—.
3   The first sound which the child writes; then the two sounds joined, and the child writes the second one, for example c—/car—.

It is important to omit the eight words whose long or diphthong vowels are spelt with only one letter. They are *he, we, be, so, no, to, do,* and *go.* Then, the teacher uses a similar technique with three sounds at a time. When short vowels are included later in the scheme, it is important to omit those words whose first two letters result in a word with a long or diphthong vowel sound. Here are some examples: *hen, wet, bed, sock, not, top, dog, got.* It is too dangerous to include them in this kind of practice. The children would be sure to form wrong associations, which they would find it difficult to unlearn.

Many children repeat the sounds they hear to help them sort them out before writing them down. This is an allowable step and one to be encouraged in preparation for the time when the children think of their own words. As a test to show the teacher whether the children recognize the sets of sounds they are writing as words, it is useful to devote an occasional lesson to mainly non-words, asking the children to say if they recognize a real word. But care must be taken to include only words already known by the children, and only combinations of sounds which exist in some English words.

Rationale and linear progression

1 The beginning of the progression is the teaching of primary consonantal phonic associations, which has been described.

2 Because it has been found that many children grasp the association principle more easily in long-vowel examples, e.g. *seat, moon, farm*, these have been listed first. The differences between short vowels, long vowels and diphthong-vowels should be clearly understood by the teacher, and explained to any child who is thought likely to benefit from the information. This is possible with more children than most teachers think.

3 Consonant diagraphs are learnt next, e.g. *fish, then*, etc. One of the lists includes 'th—' words such as '*thin*', and another one 'th—' words such as '*the*'. It may be necessary to point out that, although most voiced/ voiceless distinctions are represented by different letters, here the two different sounds are represented by the same letter-pairs, which in the spelling task is an economy.

4 Consonant blends, e.g. *pram, tent*, etc., follow the digraphs, and then irregular consonants, e.g. *bridge, catch*, etc. The three consonant categories are repeated, but this time coupled with irregular vowels, e.g. sh*oe*, br*eak*, l*augh*.

5 Although most noun plurals are one-syllable words, they are not as vital as the two-syllable words which result from the addition of the verb endings *-ing, -ed*, and *-en*. Verb modifications are therefore listed first. A similar sequence is presented, verbs with short vowels being followed by those with long or diphthong vowels. But they are grouped according to the method of adding the ending, i.e.:

 –no change to the verb stem
 –the omission of the final *-e* from the verb stem.
 –the doubling of the final consonant of the verb stem.

Irregular past tense forms are listed first, as most of them are more frequent, and have only one syllable, and contain a short vowel. Then regular one-syllable past tenses, e.g. *filled, turned*, are followed by two-syllable examples with the same spelling, e.g. *waited, mended*; and then by more one-syllable examples with an *-ed* ending but a final *-t* sound. By the time these are reached, the visual *-ed* pattern should be established.

6 After a few examples of regular noun-plurals, and all the irregular ones in the vocabulary, are listed the similarly spelt examples of the third person singular *-s* ending on verbs.

7 The rest of the programme comprises the remaining polysyllabic words, starting with the addition of *-n't* to auxiliary verbs, and then the words beginning with the schwa vowel spelt with 'a'. There are four lists of words, most of whose components have already been learnt. The frequent endings *-er, -est, -y*, and *-ies* follow. Again the sub-grouping is based on the various methods of adding endings.

8 Then follow whole words with two syllables which have not already been learnt as words, including the *-le, -et*, and *-en* endings. Days and

months continue the progression. Then come examples of further ways of spelling the final schwa sound, and another miscellaneous list. These must of course be learnt by a whole-word method.

9 Some three- and four-syllable words complete the programme. These sub-groups are based as far as possible on the position of the stress in the word. Eight words whose written form contains one more syllable than their spoken form are followed by a final list of –*ier* and –*iest* endings.

Teaching phonic spelling in a class lesson

Although it is inevitable that, in any class, spelling ability is never within a narrow range, class lessons can, and should, be given. Nobody learns nothing. The least advanced children must be encouraged to do all they can, and a little more; those in the middle range are working at their level most of the time, with mild competition from the rest; and the ability of the most advanced can be extended, to include an application of phonic information to words beyond the basic vocabulary, or to related longer words later in the phonic scheme.

Here is the sequence of activities from an actual 30-minute lesson given to a group of children whose spelling ability was within a wide range. They were between six and nine years old. The youngest had been at the school for only three months, and the oldest for about two years. They all had severe expressive language disorders: and most of them had phonological disorders, a few being mild, but more being severe. One was still finding difficulty in understanding the concept of words being composed of a sequence of identifiable sounds. His powers of concentration were stretched to their limit, and it was apparent that he was gradually grasping the idea of analysing words into sounds, associating the sounds with letters, and synthesizing these into written words. Another boy, whose phonic ability was far beyond that of most of the class, was working on his own at a more advanced level. But sometimes he was asked to join in the blackboard lesson, both for purposes of revision, and to provide a model for the other children. Most of the class were in the early stages of being able to discriminate between long vowel sounds, either between pairs of them, or threes, or fours, or fives; that is, between –*ee*– and –*oo*– (as in *moon*); or between these and –*ar*–, –*or*–, and –*ur*–.

The teacher's aim was to teach the spelling of the sound –*ee*–, spelt –*ea*–, as in '*seat*'. The only word-types used were consonant + vowel (CV), as in '*sea*'; VC, as in '*eat*' and CVC, as in '*seat*'. The only consonants used were those in which the sound was represented by one letter only, as in '*seat*', thus excluding words like '*beach*', in which the final consonant sound is represented by two letters. So the list, using all the words in the basic vocabulary which matched the necessary criteria, was limited to: *sea, tea, eat, seat, meat, read, leaf*, and *pea*.

The consonants were written on the board, in a well spaced row, and a check was made to ensure that all the children could decode them all. A list of the –*ea*– diagraph was made. The teacher added consonants to turn each -ea- into a word. A different child read each word. Then they listened to each other reading most of the words, taking turns to read one each. They were then proficient enough to read the whole list, and the more advanced children were given the more complex task of reading them in a random order, and faster; and more words such as '*beat*' and '*team*'; and the original words with an ending, such as '*eating*'. So far the teacher had done all the spelling, and the children all the reading.

Now the children did the spelling. With the row of consonants as a visual aid, each child made a given word by adding an initial or final letter, or both, to an -ea- in a newly written list. Later they repeated this but the row of consonants had been removed. The next stage was for each child to write on the board, from memory, a complete word, selected by the teacher. Gradually more responsibility was given to the children. One -ea- was left on the board. They each wrote in their books all the words as they were dictated by the teacher. Lastly, all the clues on the board were removed, and the children tried to write the words entirely from memory.

The series of lessons which followed was based on the other long vowel sounds. Before each new one was introduced, at least one familiar one was revised. Not until the primary spellings of all long vowels and diphthong vowels are throughly mastered should comparisons be made between them.

Supplementary activities
Further activities can be provided for children to use in small groups, or pairs, or individually, designed to consolidate the learning which has been started in class lessons.

Word lists are presented on cards, and arranged in such a way that phonic relationships are easily seen. The cards can be used as the basis for copying activities, for writing sentences, each of which includes at least one of the words, and for informal testing.

The same words are written separately on small cards, and kept in a series of small storage drawers, each of which is divided into three compartments. The front compartment holds all the words with the primary spelling of the vowel sound; the next holds words with all secondary spellings; and the last has all the relevant polysyllabic words. The teacher directs a child who needs a given word to the appropriate drawer.

Learning primary vowel spellings relies on the skills of auditory discrimination and phonic association. This is followed by the need to practise visual memory skills. A series of large vowel matrices give the opportunity to sort groups of words with different ways of spelling the same vowel sound.

A game resembling Lexicon is played with packs of specially made cards. Each of the three packs is designed to emphasize the use of a particular group of vowels: long vowels, short vowels, and diphthongs. The vowel cards are coloured according to these distinctions; and the

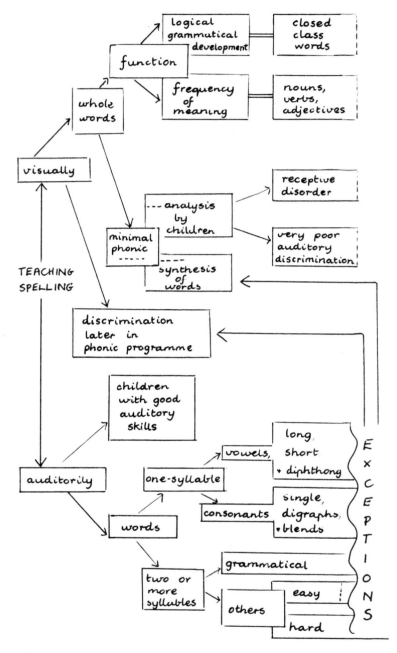

Figure 7.2   Teaching spelling: a summary of the chapter

consonant cards according to nasal, and oral voiced and voiceless groupings.

A series of phonic word grids is used with children who need practice in seeing differences rapidly.

Some teachers use word-books, with or without stepped indexing. In order to avoid confusing associations, there are three extra pages, for words beginning with '*th-*', '*sh-*', and '*ch-*'.

Testing

A pair of tests, sampling whole-word spelling and phonic spelling abilities, have been devised. They provide information about a child's individual learning style, and give the teacher guidance about where in either or both schemes a child can most fruitfully begin.

Conclusion

Anyone who can spell all the words in the phonic programme has learnt the core vocabulary necessary for basic written communication. It gives children who have specific auditory and/or visual difficulties a logical progression which provides the maximum opportunity for overcoming them. Gradually, as a child's knowledge of phonic associations accumulates, he applies it more and more to the process of reading. The goal of phonic spelling has been extended, and reached once more. More reading improves spelling ability still further, and literacy continues to increase.

8 Art and Craft

Children with severe language disorders usually have less difficulty in the visual modality than in the auditory one. Despite this, and despite average intelligence, their visual perception is still immature. They do not readily see the global shape of an object or a picture; instead they notice specific minor visual features to the exclusion of the major one; or unimportant details in photographs or drawings. Teachers discover that they must present all information unambiguously, and all visual aids as simply as possible, with no irrelevant detail. The visual perception of a language disordered child is reflected in his inability to draw as well as his normal peers. He draws arms protruding from ears; fingers, if any, like innumerable spikes; houses with windows beyond the walls; cars with two wheels at the top, and the other two at the bottom of the body. All these features are to be expected in the drawing of a much younger child.

A teacher new to a class of language disordered children soon finds other common difficulties, such as poor body-image, immature fine motor control, and minimal hand/eye coordination. Pencils, scissors, and other tools are used clumsily; and even if a child knows the relationships between the parts of an object, he may be unable to show this in his drawing. He often has little sense of visual rhythm.

Aims and activities

It is not because education in the manual arts is considered unimportant that so far no systematic curriculum in this area has been devised at the John Horniman School. On the contrary it could be because the reasons for teaching them are related to so many other curriculum areas. Drawing, painting and making are all essential in the development of representational ability in the language disordered child. They contribute towards the fulfilment of his need for creativity. They provide practice for his organization of himself and his materials. They improve his self-perception and coordination. They help him in his factual and conceptual learning, and provide a foundation for him to appreciate the design of environmental objects as a basis for choice of his own possessions later in life.

Art and craft sessions are sometimes assigned to the reinforcement of ideas introduced into other curriculum areas, such as environmental studies. Effective visual aids can be produced to emphasize the essential parts of a process (such as bread-making) or a cycle (such as rubbish disposal) or a growth pattern (such as tomatoes or beans).

The beginnings of the appreciation of art, for its own sake and in design, are included in the general discussion which precedes and follows artistic activities. Children find elements to praise in each other's work, and learn to take a pride in their own.

Provision is made in the weekly timetable for at least one painting or craft session. This may be free-standing, that is, included for its own sake: it may, however, be related in some way to another current topic. The choice of activity must depend on the spontaneity and creativity of each classroom teacher. If she has specialized in the teaching of art, she finds no difficulty in sharing her enthusiasm with her language disordered class. She uses her materials adventurously, and this provides a good example for the children. But a teacher with no specialist knowledge must not be inhibited by this apparent disadvantage. She can share genuinely in the delight of creating, which is one of the major outcomes of any art or craft session. When she has a creative idea, the time to share it is the present, or at least within a week, because in a few months' time it will probably have gone stale. This is also what happens, unfortunately, to ideas which, because they have been successful, are repeated. They sometimes lose their initial impact. So inventiveness is essential if art lessons are to remain alive.

Most language disordered children who have experienced difficulties in spoken expression during their pre-school years, have developed some kind of gesture system. Some of them, predominantly those with a receptive language disorder, also make use of drawing as a major means of communication. The pencil of such a child serves as a necessary means of self-expression. He may also have discovered the usefulness of a rubber. He draws a boat with a fisherman on its deck. He rubs out the fishing line and rod, replacing them at a different angle, with a fish drawn at the end of the line. Or he draws a queue of people at a bus-stop. After some kind of representation of a gust of wind, everybody's hats are rubbed out and replaced in the road because the wind has blown them away. Some children who draw fast enjoy making a series of strip-cartoons: but to others this is too cumbersome to be pleasurable. It is vital that drawing is encouraged, both as a means of communication when gesture or manual signing fails, and as a continuing means of the expression of ideas and feelings. The children who have not already learned to draw should be taught a simple method of achieving it. The provision of conventional drawings of familiar objects for copying usually serves as sufficient stimulus for more imaginative attempts. No language disordered child should be expected to decode even the simplest of written words until he both understands and uses drawings, however simple they must be. They are one of the major links between reality and arbitrary representation.

Pure enjoyment is one of the most important aims of an art lesson. Many language disordered children consider themselves as failures by the time they reach school age. As this is not a satisfactory attitude on which to build learning patterns, their self-confidence must be increased. They are pleased with their attempts to use colour, in the media of paint, or paper, or materials with other textures, such as those used in simple collage. Most individual items are displayed in the classroom, or where more people can enjoy them. But they are replaced with further work after a week, as their familiarity causes them not to be 'seen' properly after that. Sometimes the children's efforts result in decorative contributions to Christmas and other festivities. This kind of activity provides a greater opportunity for children to enjoy and admire each other's work. Cooperative tasks can be even more satisfying, being a practical example of the theory that the whole is greater than the sum of its parts. It is often a lasting thrill to know that one's smallest contribution has made a difference to a very pleasing collage or giant painting. This feeling is fed back to a language disordered child as an increased motivation for learning.

Although language disordered children may have been growing up in an orderly household, they may not have learned any self-organization skills. Some families' good intentions lead them to the assumption that, because a child has difficulty in understanding or using speech, he should not be expected to hold a knife and fork properly, to tidy up after himself, nor to be made responsible for the routine daily events in which he is involved. The painting lesson is one of the classroom situations in which this lack of expectation can be remedied. It occurs frequently enough that the routine sequence is not forgotten. The arrangement of furniture is similar enough from week to week that a constant visual pattern can be provided. The main sequence of events can always be the same. In a new class it is wise to allocate what seems a disproportionate amount of time on preparation and clearing-up. During the first few lessons the teacher gives clear instructions to individual children. Each one is responsible for one set of items: paints, water, brushes, aprons, easels, newspaper. When all these are ready for use, the real lesson can begin. A discussion follows on the subjects to be painted, appropriate colours, and a few warnings about the correct use of materials. Each child is asked to close his eyes and imagine his painting in detail. Then the activity begins.

A teacher whose class does not need to be constantly watched is wise to carry out for herself the activity she has discussed with the children. This stops her from unnecessarily interfering with the children's work. It does not allow her to be tempted to do some classroom task which is irrelevant to the current lesson. It gives her the opportunity to experience potential difficulties, and also to enjoy the results, however primitive, of the activity itself.

Later in the lesson children are more ready to welcome her comments on their work. A sensitive teacher who understands the stages through which most children progress, can judge when it is appropriate to make helpful suggestions. She encourages them to make immediate observations of, for example, the junction of arms and body; or to consider whether they can see the lower edge of the sky. It is important that this kind of instruction is given at the right moment, after a suitable time in which complete freedom is allowed. Each child must be shown that he can achieve more. The same principle applies to the use of more appropriate colours. With guidance a child can produce much more pleasing compositions.

At the end of the session, each child is responsible for the cleaning of his apron, his desk or easel, his own patch of floor, and for returning each item to a central place, from which each set is carried to its storage position by the children who prepared them at the beginning of the lesson. The whole operation is logical, fair, and a practical example of the process of organization. A class becomes so familiar with the routine that, after a few weeks, the teacher can expect the room to be prepared and tidied quickly and efficiently, with the minimum of reminders from her.

Local rules are devised: some teachers prefer a brush to be assigned to each paint-pot, rather than to each child. This is preferable in the early stages as it eliminates the need to explain how to clean the brush before another colour is used. So it allows more time for the children to paint, and less paint is wasted. Later each child can be given the responsibility for caring for his own brush. As he grows more confident he is taught how to choose between three sizes of brush to achieve different effects; and how to mix colours. As with other young children, language disordered children too can be introduced to simple variations in techniques, such as the use of damp paper; or the addition of white paint to the colours, making a more opaque form; or the provision of black or coloured paper.

Another technique which is helpful is to provide non-vocal music as a positive background to a painting lesson. The title of the piece may be related to the subject of the painting, but it need not be. Children who are initially afraid of an empty sheet of paper gain confidence as they use an empty brush for a few minutes, practising the strokes they will make with paint later. Some children paint rhythmically in time to the music, but this is not essential. The main object is to release inhibition, and to encourage relaxation and freedom. A confident teacher can introduce an occasional experiment with finger-painting, for example, spreading over the paper a small quantity of paint which has been tipped on to it.

The construction of models or toys from junk material also provides an opportunity for understanding the relationship between parts of objects, and the principles behind joining two parts together. Many language disordered children need detailed instruction in using gummed paper and glue: some children do not realize that they must lick the adhesive side of a piece of paper and not the coloured side; one child, wanting to stick a cardboard top onto a cardboard cylinder, to make a one-legged table, spread glue all over the outer surface of the cylinder, and then wondered why the required piece would not stick on top.

Other basic principles of construction can be introduced such as modelling with clay or plasticine, and weaving and basket-making and needlework. And the mathematical concept of area can be brought to the children's attention by exercises in all kinds of pattern-making. Making mobiles introduces the idea of three-dimensional art of a different kind.

A wide variety of activities, each approached in an ordered and purposeful way, contribute towards the fulfilment of the children's present and future diverse needs.

9   Educational drama

Verbal language is a sophisticated form of representation. A young child with a severe disorder of language must be helped to approach its complexity via a route which, for normally developing children, is natural. Simple representational skills are part of most children's activities. But, as with other aspects of skill acquisition in language disordered children, no assumptions can be made. Although, by the time they are old enough to go to school, some may have learned to imitate and pretend, and to recognize toys as representatives of adult tools and other equipment, many have not done so. Because they usually possess an outwardly undamaged physique, adults often expect them to be comparably mature in other areas. Because their presenting disorder is in the area of language acquisition, remediators have to include the teaching of the concept of representation as an important part of the school curriculum. Some of these children have not observed the stable factors in their environment. Their skills of perception must be increased. Perhaps the world they know is almost as small as that of a baby learning to walk. Even within this world they find it hard to differentiate between unchanging and changing factors. This leads to misunderstandings and confusion. They must be guided towards a practical awareness, not only of the physical properties of their surroundings, but also of the world of feelings, including their own. Their attention must also be drawn to ways of responding to everyday occurrences. They need to learn the concept and the importance of social cooperation, which helps each one of them to a greater understanding of himself and his own personality.

Some of the aims of this method, devised by Margaret Campkin, are to train attention and perception, in order to encourage greater environmental understanding and the formation of social concepts. Movement skills are also trained, so that tension is reduced and relaxation encouraged. Throughout each session the comprehensive superordinate aim of practising the use of language should be seen. The children take the teacher's role, giving instructions, and answering questions; and they share with her the opportunities for learning about mutual trust, pretending, and caring for others. The items described as 'language activities', near the end of each session, emphasize these aspects more specifically. Occasionally a few minutes of original creative work concludes the session.

A weekly session, lasting 35 minutes, comprising activities which achieve this comprehensive aim, is described as educational drama. The session only rarely includes the kind of activity which prepares for a performance of some kind. Time is so scarce that it cannot usually be afforded for such specific preparation. A large, well ventilated room is recommended. The children and teacher all wear the same clothing as for physical education, and preferably work in bare feet.

Attention control

The training of perception demands a degree of attention control. This is achieved by implicit rules of taking turns. A child who is not attending when it is his turn to do something, does not hear his name called and therefore misses his turn.

The manual sign system gives additional clues to the children who need them. As the use of signs is gradually withdrawn, greater responsibility for attention to auditory cues is laid on the children.

It is important that a consistent and limited vocabulary is used. The aim in drama is not so much to extend vocabulary as to make full use of what is already understood.

Warm-up

Although the first main part of each session comprises relaxation activities, these are preceded by a systematic warm-up routine, which is intended to have physical and mental effects. Each child works first with his feet, ankles, and knees; then using his spine, shoulders and neck; hands; and lastly head and neck. As he listens to the teacher's instructions about specific parts of the body, and simultaneously imitates her movements, he is learning how the parts of his body fit together, and the relevant noun- and verb-vocabulary. As the children move all together, they feel secure within the group. Their muscles are loosened up and are ready for the next part of the lesson.

Relaxation

A common hindrance to the early classroom adjustment of children with severe language disorders is their lack of confidence, which manifests itself in increased bodily tension. There are aspects of their lives in which they have experienced stress. When they try to use a pencil their grip is so tight, and often unsuitable, that flowing handwriting is impossible. It is of paramount importance to reduce this tension. This is usually achieved by encouraging them to become even more tense, by pushing, stretching or squeezing, and then to stop suddenly. A state of relaxation is induced. Although it is a difficult art to learn, it is an essential part of their education if this is to prove enjoyable and useful. Physical relaxation leads eventually to mental relaxation and thence to a more receptive mind.

The increase of tension is more easily practised, initially, in pairs. Children push each other's backs or palms; pull each other over a chalk line on the floor, or, while lying prone on the floor, stretch to reach each other, without moving their bodies along the floor. In later sessions they are ready for individual activities, such as lifting imaginary weights, or shadow boxing.

The rest of the session

The warm-up and relaxation activities are included in every session. The other three main aspects of the drama scheme are used selectively. Sometimes the teacher concentrates on several different exercises with one main aim, training either perception; or a specific aspect of language; or creative skills: sometimes she chooses one or two activities from each category. As she works, she discovers still further permutations of her original ideas, and the children are also encouraged to contribute their own.

Perceptual activities
Non-pitched percussion instruments are introduced for the purpose of improving gross auditory discrimination. Having listened to each stimulus, the children learn to respond by moving in distinctly different ways. A sequence of two, and, later, three, different instruments provides a much more complex task. Subtler response is called for in further ways: moving in a very small space when the instrument is played quietly, or using the whole room when it is played loudly; or, instead of moving, making one's body into different shapes which correspond to the instrument being played.

Listening to gross environmental sounds is another method of increasing auditory awareness. The teacher or a child opens a door, plays a note on the piano or eats an imaginary meal from a real plate with real cutlery. But the other children either have their eyes closed, or they have their backs to the source of the sound. The range of sounds to be identified can be extended by the tape recording of those normally impossible to be introduced into the classroom.

And children are encouraged to experiment with long speech sounds, like 'oo . . . . .', 'sh . . . . .', and 'mmm . . . . .'. They think carefully what each one reminds them of, such as the wind, and in some this elicits a longer verbal response.

A 'feely' box contains items which provide practice in *haptic* perception. Each child feels one item slowly and carefully, and as he does this, he names the item and talks about its function. Tactile perception is heightened by feeling successive items of clothing, and moving in ways which correspond to the adjectives used to describe each one, such as 'soft', 'scratchy' or 'heavy'.

Specific language activities: from imitation, through representation to communication

Many of the tasks already described give opportunities for experiencing the meanings of words. And children can begin to learn how to trust each other; how to show a variety of personal feelings in changes in facial expressions and in the tone of voice; to become aware of the movements made by other people carrying out tasks which can be mimed; and how to pretend to be those people. Greater demands are made on the children as they practise working in pairs. A blindfolded child is led around the room by another one. Later still, minor obstacles can be placed around the room. And the seeing child can help the blindfolded one to sit on a chair or on the floor.

Mirroring tasks are begun by palm-to-palm contact, which ensures that partners face each other throughout all the movements initiated by the one who leads by applying pressure onto his partner's hands. Once the concept is grasped, and turning movements are included, imitation need not be quite so exact.

Shadowing is more difficult, as the children cannot see each other's faces: the follower can see only the back of the leader, and the leader cannot monitor his partner's movements at all.

'Pretending' is a difficult concept for language disordered children to learn. At first it is applied to the expression of basic feelings, for example, happiness, sadness, anger and fear. These same feelings can be expressed within a single greeting, 'Hello!' Later the children practise the miming of other people's actions.

When children have become used to working in pairs, they can enter group situations. They join hands in fours or fives and travel around the room showing that they are happy, or afraid, or tired. All the groups work at the same task. Later, each one is assigned a different task, and the demand for concentration is increased.

Creative activities

Not until a complete class is capable of an acceptable standard in most of the preceding activities can they begin to take differing roles in an 'acting' task. There need be no speech in an initial one. One such occasion was the miming of a cricket match. Nine children played indoors with a substantial ruler for a bat, and a very soft ball. After a few minutes they dispensed with the two properties, and continued the game. They concentrated so well that they all followed the imaginary ball with their eyes, wherever it was bowled, hit or caught. The result gave great satisfaction to all the children. It could not have been achieved without much preliminary work. If and when speaking parts are assumed, and feelings and facts of an imaginary person begin to be expressed, the teaching task of this level of drama has been achieved.

10   A movement system based on the Margaret Morris Movement, Special Schools' Syllabus

It has often been noted that, when language disordered children are participating in a movement lesson, they give the impression that they are physically handicapped. Many of them are so disorientated, uncoordinated, and generally clumsy when moving, that it is hard to believe that they are the same children who look otherwise physically normal. They resemble the 10-year-old boy described in Gordon and McKinlay's book, *Helping clumsy children* (1980) p.63. Asked to stand on his left leg and hold his right leg up behind him he shows that:

1 He cannot stand on one leg.
2 He does not know his left from his right side.
3 He cannot tell up from down, nor front from back.
4 He has lack of body symmetry, poor limb girdle organization, fixation and control.
5 He has immature or poor balance and equilibrium reactions.
6 He has excessive associated movements.
7 He has increase or decrease in muscle tone.
8 He has auditory memory or sequencing difficulties.
9 He shows a sense of failure through a refusal or attempt to distract the examiner.

These nine points describe a greater proportion of children with expressive than with receptive language disorders.

Requirements for a structured programme

During the first few years of John Horniman School's existence, the teachers attempted to help the children to learn the physical skills appropriate to their age-group. It soon became apparent that this was impossible. The children were not ready to use apparatus in physical education lessons. They could neither skip nor turn a rope nor jump over one: they could not throw or catch balls, of whatever size. The simplest of playground games demanded a maturity which none of them possessed. They could not hop, so they could not skip. They could not organize their bodies to jump with both feet. Some could run, but not efficiently. They could all walk, but many in an ungainly fashion.

Gradually other skills were being structured in such a way that no child was asked to begin at a stage beyond his natural ability. But the structuring of physical skills was postponed, until time could be spent in obtaining and organizing the expert knowledge which would be necessary for such a project. Meanwhile country dancing was attempted, energetically and enthusiastically, but learning remained minimal.

We searched for a system of physical education which was logical. We needed to be able to teach each sub-skill separately. Preferably items should be graded in order of difficulty. There should be a number of cues to memory which could be removed gradually. It must be possible to give simple instructions using the minimum of vocabulary.

Margaret Morris Movement was discovered by a teacher at an adult education class. She was attracted by Schubert's music, and by the mixed group of participants. By the end of a year of weekly classes, she realized that this was the system which should be introduced at the school. A similarity was seen between it and the programme then being devised for pre-school language disordered children by Cooper, Moodley and Reynell (1978), and described by them in *Helping Language Development*. Its theoretical basis provided a pattern for the theoretical use of Margaret Morris Movement. There were definite parallels between the two systems. Reynell's model began with attention control; then, through verbal comprehension and visual perception, approached concept formation and symbolic understanding. Simultaneously, visuo-motor association and motor function linked the concepts with expressive language; all these processes were completed in the integration of language performance. Thus, before producing a self-generated utterance, a child must learn to attend, to listen, to look, to think symbolically and creatively, and to construct a sentence in which to communicate his meaning. The physical exercises in Margaret Morris Movement require a similar progression of learning processes: attention, auditory and visual perception combined, and the formation of the concepts of body awareness and of its position in space; the ability to organize one's own body to imitate the positions and movements of another body, the ability to move the organized parts, and to coordinate their movements with each other. The processes which parallel expressive language and language performance integration are the improvisation of new movements and sequences and their execution. These stages are not always reached. But every process preceding them is part of the necessary preparation for them. Margaret Morris herself said, in relation to teaching the exercises to children with physical and mental handicaps, 'The feeling of achievement, however slight, is what is so important in making further progress possible.'

The overall structure of Margaret Morris Movement resembles a pyramid, in which over 300 exercises are organized within 10 colour grades, the exercises in each grade being based on those in the previous grades, which in turn are based on those which constitute the foundation of the system, described as the Basic grade. This grade comprises 50 exercises, and variations on most of them. With language disordered children we are concerned with only 20 of these. This selected group comprises a miniature version of the essentials of the whole system. Each

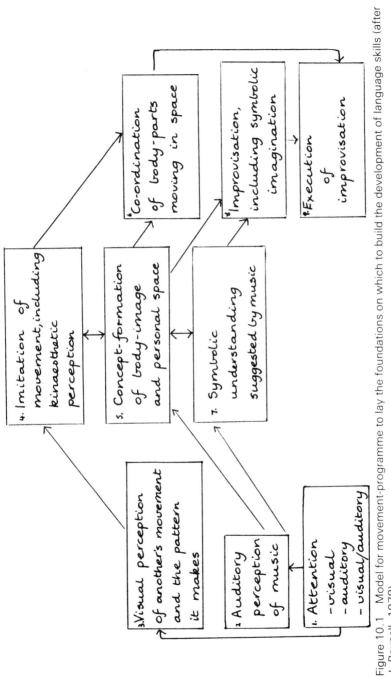

Figure 10.1 Model for movement-programme to lay the foundations on which to build the development of language skills (after J. Reynell, 1978).

exercise has its own anatomical and physiological aim. It is also 'a balanced composition in itself, ensuring harmonious development of the body'. (White, 1980). Both harmony and melody of movements exist within the exercises.

Margaret Morris, as an expert dancer, began the system by devising the exercises which are now in the middle of the 10 colour grades. Then, realizing that untrained bodies would need a gradual approach to these, she 'unravelled' them, by simplifying them, and continuing to simplify the simplifications, until they became accessible to anyone with the motivation to begin. During a few years' experience of using these with handicapped children, we have naturally had to modify them still further. It is, however, always preferable that teachers themselves learn the original Basic exercises, and devise their own ways of modifying them.

Three main features of Margaret Morris Movement

There are three features about the Margaret Morris Movement system which, taken together, distinguish it from all other systems of movement. There is a three-fold emphasis: on breathing with all the exercises; on spinal mobility; and on the opposition of arms and legs.

– Specific breathing types and patterns are suggested: the types are described as deep, expiratory, and synchronized; the breathing rhythms are consistent within and between exercises, so that they gradually become 'natural', and do not need specific learning when an unfamiliar exercise is first introduced. The aim is to ventilate all portions of the lungs. This develops full pulmonary capacity, and therefore increases stamina and a sense of well-being.

– The full range of spinal mobility is developed, including the lateral movements of the thorax and pelvis. The spine is mobilized, and posture is improved.

– Basic opposition positions of arms and legs accentuate natural movements. They strengthen and limber the muscles used in everyday living.

Not only does Margaret Morris Movement possess its own intrinsic logical structure; not only does it parallel the theoretical model (Cooper *et al.*, *op. cit.*) used as the basis of the Wolfson language intervention programme; not only does it have its three-fold special emphasis; but the system also fits our requirements regarding the teaching of separate sub-skills; the grading of exercises in order of difficulty; cues to memory which can be gradually removed; and a minimum vocabulary. No other system discovered so far has fitted our needs so exactly.

Margaret Morris's own work with children

Margaret Morris (1891-1980) was born in London, but spent her early childhood in France. She studied ballet, and rebelled against what she considered to be the artificialities of the Italian ballet, and began to evolve her own system of dance technique. She had not only an artistic purpose in doing this, but also a personal physical reason. As a child she had had a curvature of the spine, and this was cured, but by such boring exercises that she vowed that she would devise some of her own, which would be both useful and interesting. She soon realized that the exercises could be enjoyed for their own sake. She also trained as a physiotherapist, and eventually adapted her exercises for many kinds of uses. Some have been included in sports training; others have been modified for use before and after childbirth; and others for young children. These, known as 'Health Play' exercises, are not as suitable for language disordered children as the 'Basic' ones. Neither are the Children's Grades generally used with them, as they are more complex and less definite.

Margaret Morris taught handicapped children herself, in various parts of England and Scotland. Their class teachers reported improvements in other classroom skills, which they attributed in part to the exercises. But she found that the local education authorities, in the period just before the Second World War, did not acquire the necessary enthusiasm to publicize the effect they could have. Joan White (1980) suggested other possibilities for the non-inclusion of the Margaret Morris Movement method in the educational world: her talents were widespread, but she was not able to make optimum use of publicity methods; the war and other time coincidences appear to have militated against her; she was well ahead of her time; other physical education systems had been imported from other countries, and Margaret Morris was British! Margaret Morris once predicted the possibility that the value of her system might be recognized more widely after her death. It may be that this prediction is beginning to come true.

Margaret Morris Movement aims, related to the 20 exercises and to the needs of language disordered children

There follows a description of the specific aims of the Margaret Morris system of movement, as set out by Margaret Morris herself and interpreted by the administrator of the Movement, with examples of some exercises which carry out these aims, and their application to the needs of language disordered children. For a list of these exercises see Table 10.1.

We cannot live without breathing. We normally give no thought to the act of breathing. There was a time when Margaret Morris believed it was not important to suggest specific ways of breathing. But after 10 years' experience of teaching her exercises she became convinced that better

Table 10.1: The special Schools' Syllabus (selected from the Basic Grade in 1979).

1	Run and balance	11	Aeroplane balance
2	Run and limber	12	Head stretch and relax
3	Hop	13	Arm circling
4	Walk	14	Basic arm
5	Inner border raising	15	Standing (and sitting) stretching
6	Heel raising	16	Side stretching
7	Knee bending	17	Quadriceps stretching
8	Easy breathing	18	Tension and relaxation
9	Breathing progression	19	Leg-swinging
10	Balance progression	20	Scissors

results were obtained when the breathing rhythm was taught as an integral part of each one. The reason for this is that in normal unconscious breathing, only a part of the full lung capacity is used: but it is important that the greater the capacity of the lungs that is used, the more oxygen is absorbed, and the more work the muscles are able to perform. More waste carbon dioxide is released, together with more energy. Practising deep breathing develops stamina, prevents infection and burns up excessive fat. One of the ways in which to encourage it is to teach the function of the abdominal wall in effective deep breathing. Conscious relaxation of the abdominal muscles when breathing in, and their conscious contraction when breathing out is a useful habit to form. They assist the action of the diaphragm in releasing the maximum amount of stale air, during expiration, and help it to relax in order to allow the maximum inspiration of fresh air. The exercise known as Easy Breathing includes interesting head and arm movements, and knee-bending: but its main purpose is to practise full inspiration while stretching the arms up, and expiration during the relaxation of the body. And the three variations of Breathing Progression teach the increasing expansion of the lungs. The four parts of the Balance Progression are some of the exercises which aim to strengthen the abdominal wall.

But the abdominal muscles are not the only ones which are strengthened. All the major muscle-groups in the body are given strong work through the repertoire of exercises. And at the same time all joints are mobilized, not only those which are normally in everyday use. The ball and socket arm joints are rotated, in Arm-circling; in Leg-swinging, the normal movement of each hip-joint is exaggerated; and most joints and muscles of the upper limbs are worked in the Basic Arm exercise. In the Head Stretch and Relax exercise, the neck muscles are strengthened, and the cervical region of the upper spine is mobilized. The three exercises described as Stretching, that is Standing or Sitting Stretching, Side Stretching, and *Quadriceps* Stretching, give strong work to all the spinal

Plate 10.1 A Margaret Morris Movement stretching exercise is being attempted.

flexors and extensors, to the intercostal muscles, and the hamstrings and quadriceps. In other exercises, all parts of the body are given the opportunity to stretch and relax. One exercise for the specific practice of Tension and Relaxation is known by that name. It develops the conscious relaxation of the whole of the upper part of the body.

Particular attention is given to the feet, not only in Running, 'Hopping' (the Margaret Morris Movement description of the kind of 'skipping' which cannot be achieved until hopping is mastered) and Scissors (jumping) exercises, but also in those for Heel-raising, Knee-bending, and Inner Border (of the feet) Raising. The ankles are strengthened, and also the transverse and longitudinal arches of the feet.

Emphases on spinal and abdominal control and accuracy of foot movements lead to improvement in posture, and thence to the ability to balance. Although this is a factor in several exercises already mentioned, it is specifically practised in others, such as Run and Balance, and Aeroplane Balance.

Language-disordered children often hear the names of parts of the body when spoken instructions for the exercise-sequences are being given. They learn about body articulation by practising the movement of specific parts. They also move around the room, and experience different directions and limitations. In some exercise-sequences movement round the room is alternated with movement in one place, as in the Running and some of the Walking exercises. In Hopping and Scissors the children are encouraged to make the fullest possible use of the space above them by using the floor as a springboard.

Importance is laid on rhythm in all the exercises. The music is used as the stimulus for this, and also as a unifying force. The children gradually learn that their personal satisfaction in performing an exercise is increased if they are keeping in time with the rest of the class. In order to conform to the most common natural timing of the class, it is advisable to ask the pianist to watch the children, or to use a cassette-recorder with a control that changes the pitch, and consequently the speed, of the music. There are exercises for normal walking and slow walking, and an even slower exercise known as the Slow Motion Walk. This needs an increasing degree of control, greater than most of these children have. It may sound too great a challenge to coordinate breathing with movement, at the same time as movement with music, but it is achieved by some children. They then find that breathing in time with the music helps them to move in time with it. So what has been an added hindrance is gradually converted to an additional cue.

Margaret Morris's final aim is continuity. When a coordinated body with mobilized joints and strengthened muscles can move freely and stop at will, in time with its own breathing, and in time with the music and with other people, using controlled tension and relaxation, the feel for continuity begins to grow. So does the confidence which many language disordered children initially lack. Their physical achievement contributes to their belief that other challenges can be grasped and difficulties overcome. Margaret Morris Movement is thus a physical lever to an expanding mind and a freedom of spirit, all of them necessary for future growth.

Modification methods

There are a number of ways in which exercises from the Basic Grade can be modified for use with children whose physical skills are limited. They must be taught in several stages, each one being introduced only after some improvement is evident in the mastery of the previous one. This may mean that the complete exercise is reached only after a few weeks, or even longer. Part of an exercise can be presented temporarily as if it were a complete one. For example, Heel-raising is, basically, 'Walk, two, three, together; up and down and . . . ' repeated several times. Teaching the exercise can be broken down into three stages: walking in time with the music; walking for three steps, closing feet together, and waiting for four beats; standing with feet together and practising heel-raising, up for two beats and down for two beats. When the second and third stages are mastered separately, walking and heel-raising are combined in an alternating sequence. This is a worthwhile achievement.

The Easy Breathing sequence is taught very gradually. Children face each other across a circle. They try to breathe in for four beats and out for four. Then, starting with their chins on their chests, they raise their heads for four beats and lower it for the next four. If any of them remember to breathe simultaneously, they are praised. Similarly, beginning with knees slightly bent, they straighten them during four beats and bend them again during the next four. This time anyone who remembers to synchronize breathing or head-movements, or both, with knee changes, is praised. Finally, arm-movements are practised. The ultimate aim is to synchronize head-, knee-, arm-movements and breathing.

The Basic Arm exercise is approached gradually: first, without any accompanying music; then, at half speed; the head movement is practised separately; arms and head are moved at half speed, then full speed. Not until this stage is breathing mentioned. More ambitious children occasionally attempt the adult version, that is, moving the head 'right, left, up, down', followed by 'left, right, up, down', thus starting alternate sequences by facing in opposite directions. Even then, there is no need to label directions like this. They are just as easily described as 'wall, gate, ceiling, floor'.

Music

Although live piano music is the preferred movement stimulus, records and tapes are available, and constitute a viable alternative. Franz Schubert was the composer whose music Margaret Morris originally chose. Other pianist composers have since contributed alternative tunes. In many special school classes these suggested tunes are used; but in others, other kinds of music are substituted. Where this is so, it is important that the teacher chooses music which is suitable in rhythm, quality and length. An exercise designed to be accompanied by a tune in duple or quadruple time cannot be performed as satisfactorily with a tune in triple time. The music, of whatever kind, should match the high creative standard of the exercises. And each tune should begin and end at the same time as the exercise. Planning is essential. When a class of children has become familiar with a specific exercise, they sometimes enjoy performing it in time to a metronome. But often the teacher finds that she needs the music to enable her to give a well-phrased example to the class.

Space

A large room, which should be well ventilated, is essential: or, a sandy beach. The teacher and children wear clothing which allows free movement; and usually they prefer their feet to be bare, as this ensures that they reap full benefit from specific foot exercises, and are able to control balance more efficiently. When the class is held indoors, one or more lights seem to improve the motivation of all concerned in it. A teacher who can use manual signs where appropriate has in her hands a further 'removable clue'.

Lesson plan

In the Basic instruction book is a suggested lesson plan, which is followed by most teachers with any kind of class. It is based on logic and experience. Each lesson begins with free movement, such as easy running, to warm up both the muscles and the mind. Walking and posture work follow, to enable the class to regain breath control. Then special 'deep breathing' exercises increase energy before more strenuous work. In a general class, specific opposition exercises (Basic Greek Positions, described below) are done next, as they require a high degree of concentration. Arms and legs move naturally in opposition to each other. By accentuating these movements, most of the muscles used in daily living are strengthened and limbered. Such exercises are taught to language disordered children only after they have become familiar with a large number of the simple sequences. When they are included, they are enjoyed as an extra challenge. Children know that they are not expected to learn them quickly, so when a small part of one is achieved, there is great rejoicing!

Balance exercises are also difficult, but one is usually included next. Children are surprised that they cannot balance easily, but after constant practice they improve. This visible improvement is often manifested in the child's attitude to life. He seems to gain greater personal control.

Time is usually allowed for at least one mobility exercise. These include many varieties of stretching, and should therefore not appear too early in a lesson. Specific joints are mobilized, and specific muscle-groups strengthened. The children classify these exercises into categories relating to each part of the body: head, arms, body, and legs. They learn to turn, stretch, circle, swing and jump. Some sequences are short and are therefore repeated several times; but others are longer, and require more memorizing.

Basic Greek positions

Many exercises in higher grades are based on the Greek positions, which were collected by Raymond Duncan from Greek vases. He taught them to his sister, Isadora, in an attempt to help her to evolve a specific dance technique. He also taught them to Margaret Morris, who made more definite use of them. She recognized their therapeutic and aesthetic value: that, when the positions were held, they used every muscle in the body; and that they fulfilled her criterion of perfection of design. Even the first Greek position, included in the Basic grade of the system, is too great a challenge for most of the children with whom we are concerned; but a beginning can be made by some. With feet apart, on a wide base, they practise alternating arm movements, and the contrast between relaxation and tension in the bending and stretching of the arms. Separately they practise a Greek position knee-bend, then straightening and bending the knees while taking the next step. Sometimes they want to try the arm-changing and stepping movements simultaneously. Although they do not often succeed in retaining the opposition of arms and legs, they gradually and perceptibly improve. A trained observer in a class can, by watching attempts at this exercise alone, correctly judge which children have had the longer Margaret Morris Movement experience. It can only safely be included by teachers who themselves have learned far more of the system than the exercises selected for handicapped children.

Improvisation

Ideally every session should finish with a few minutes' improvisation. It can be introduced simply, and based on a feature of one of the set exercises. The children are given an idea, 'think of a lot of different ways of moving your arms', 'think how many different parts of your body can move', or 'listen to the music. It is telling you how to move – fast? slowly? roughly? gently?', 'how high can you spring, and how can you get higher still?', 'pretend to be a cat, or the wind'. . . . They sit while they listen to the music being played once, and the next time they move. So that they have more space, and so that they can watch each other's performance, they divide into two groups, one group's turn following the other. But before the quietening end of a session, they all perform together again. This opportunity for creativity should be included at the expense of another set exercise. An encouraging teacher finds unexpected individual resources among the children. Those who are shy at first gain enough confidence that they look forward to producing their own movement ideas. Others, who begin with unimaginative plain running, gradually modify this by introducing other steps, and variations in ways of moving other parts of their bodies. One eight-year-old boy tried to imitate a ballet dancer he had seen on the television. . . .

Choice of exercises

It is difficult to suggest a suitable number of exercises for inclusion within a 30-minute lesson. This varies according to the experience of the teacher and children, according to degrees of enthusiasm and behaviour, and even according to what activity has preceded or will follow the movement lesson. It is usually desirable to concentrate on running, walking and breathing for a few successive sessions, say in about four or five different exercises. When these become more familiar, they can be done more quickly, and then more time is available for more complex items. A teacher must not expect too high a standard, or become despondent if no immediate success is apparent. Some children seem to make minimal progress at first, and later surprise themselves and their friends with more rapid improvement.

Variations

Variations to some exercises are described in the instructions, but these do not need to be taught in the same session as the original item. They can be held back until many sessions later, and can, if necessary, be introduced as entirely new exercises, thus increasing those in a class's repertoire to a seemingly greater number.

Teaching methods

Although it is not possible to require correct breathing all the time, it is wise to mention it frequently. Some language-disordered children find it very difficult to understand the concept of breathing in and out. It is, after all, invisible. Comparisons with balloons are sometimes helpful, but unless a teacher's vocabulary is exact, and sentences prepared in advance, she may find them a hindrance. The words 'out' and 'in' in this context are even more troublesome than usual.

A teacher gradually reduces the clues she gives, so that more and more responsibility for memory and accuracy is being placed on the children. At first, clear and brief instructions are spoken as the teacher performs the exercise. When hands and arms are not part of the exercise itself, manual signs can be made simultaneously. The music is played throughout, but either the teacher's voice can be faded out, or her own movement; and then the other. Children are thus forced into looking or listening more carefully. Eventually, some are able to perform complete exercises with no reminders from the teacher. It is not necessary to include 'left' and 'right' in instructions. 'One' and 'the other' can describe feet; and 'this side' and 'the other side' can indicate relevant sides of the body or of the room. At a more advanced stage, 'left' and 'right' can be deliberately included, but preferably only when they are thoroughly understood in other contexts. As children, and adults, mirror movements, it is important for the teacher to remember, if she is including these two direction words, that she must lift up her own right arm when she is instructing the children to lift up their left arms. And she must not include spoken instructions about diagonally opposite limbs.

Some teachers find that a class responds well to different formations for different exercises; for example, facing across a circle for symmetrical exercises, and in lines down the room for some, and across the room for others. If this is done, it should be consistent, as children tend to use it as another memory cue.

Record-keeping

Although it would be interesting and useful to keep full records of every child's response to every exercise in every lesson, this is usually impracticable. It is more reasonable to expect oneself to monitor closely just one aspect of one or two exercises in each session. It is, nevertheless, advisable to list at the beginning of each term the exercises one hopes to include, and to use this as the basis of each lesson's plan, and also as a record of what was actually done. If the teacher decides to base an occasional lesson on the children's own choice of exercises, she should arrange these into an acceptable order during the first few minutes of the session. This avoids the difficulty of two strenuous exercises being performed in quick succession.

Children's response

The children's response to Margaret Morris Movement is summarized by a nine-year-old boy's 'I want to see the other bits'. He had begun to see similarities between some of the exercises he had been learning for about two years. He had tried to do those in which two simpler exercises had been combined. He presumably realized that there were further possibilites, and when shown a few of them, immediately wanted to try them himself.

Children are to be found practising on their own, while waiting for a lesson to begin, or in their free time in the playground. They seem to understand that improvement is always possible: some are very aware of their own difficulties, and try to overcome them. They are very pleased when they recognize that their performance in an exercise is better than before.

Teachers' evaluations

A teacher's evaluation of the improvement in a child is related not only to his physical skill, but also to attention-control, body awareness, memory and self-confidence. All these improvements have been noted.

The Margaret Morris Movement system was introduced to two teachers in another school, whose pupils, between the ages of three and eight, had a wide range of problems, though mainly moderate: those included hearing loss, maladjustment, physical handicap, language disorder, and limited intelligence. One of these teachers favoured a free approach to dance, while the other was keen to learn the rudiments of a movement system which was structured. A year later they wrote:

> We lean more and more towards the artistic side. You cannot ignore the pleasure which this gives the children. We now find that the structured and free approaches complement each other well. The children love the structure of Margaret Morris Movement, and it does not hold all the confusion that they find in other dance-lessons. We have also noticed an improvement in the quality of their dance movements and in their creativity now that they have a basic repertoire of movements to give them confidence. (P. Garthwaite, 1982, personal communication.)

When Margaret Morris herself taught her exercises regularly to several groups of children with special needs, she suggested, 'Teach what the children can do easily, even if ineffectually, to establish confidence, and let them feel the joy of moving with the music'. More than this is a bonus.

Background story for children

In some schools the Margaret Morris Movement lesson is described as dancing, or movement. But in those where the full title of the system can be used, children are interested to hear about Margaret Morris herself. Her story can be told simply:

'A long time ago, a baby girl was born. Her mother and father called her Margaret. The baby's father was Mr Morris, and her mother was Mrs Morris, so the baby's name was Margaret Morris.

When Margaret was a baby she liked moving. She listened to music and she moved her arms and her legs and her head. When she was a little girl she liked dancing. She went on a stage, and a lot of people went to see her dancing. When Margaret was a bigger girl, she liked dressing up. She put her mother's old clothes on, and she pretended to be a bird or the wind. And Margaret liked drawing and painting. Sometimes she painted pictures of herself dressing up and dancing. She didn't like counting or spelling.

When Margaret was a young woman, she said, "I will teach some other women and men how to dance, and they can dance with me." She taught them to dance, and then they all danced together. Then the men and women all said, "We will teach some other people how to dance with us." So a lot more people danced together.

When Margaret was older, she like to watch people doing Margaret Morris Movement. She said, "I hope there will always be children and grown-up people who will dance like this." She asked some of her friends to write down how to do the dances. And here they are in a book. So we can do them too!'

11 Music through colour: Musicolour

Childrens with severe specific language disorders find that all aspects of language are difficult to learn. They have parallel problems in music: in its appreciation, its understanding and its performance. Their reactions are slow, particularly in the auditory modality. They find it difficult to pay attention, and their powers of concentration are limited. So are all the skills necessary in musical education: auditory discrimination, auditory memory, and rhythmic sense. The coordination necessary for playing any instrument, and for singing, is immature. These children cannot usually sing in tune, nor can they remember words of songs, or articulate them rhythmically.

Leonard Bernstein has made detailed comparisons between spoken and musical language. There is a one-to-one correspondence between the phoneme and the note; the word and the bar; the sentence and the musical phrase; and the paragraph and the melody. Just as language disordered children need very systematic instruction in language skills, so a similar approach is necessary in music. Our aims are to provide, at a very basic level, opportunities for the appreciation and creation of music, linked with structured tuition in its 'literacy'. A live concert, with children's participation, if it were available, would be an ideal situation for the means to achieve all aspects of this three-fold aim. Since such opportunities are rare, we must provide the best possible environment for this to develop.

Listening to music can train attention and increase the concentration span: it can improve the auditory skills of perception, discrimination and memory. Making music gives practice in motor coordination, and can increase social awareness and cooperation. The appreciation and performance aspects are linked by a systematic scheme which attempts to provide opportunities for understanding the basic structure of the art. When the children are given the tools for expression, they gradually discover they have ideas to express.

Exploring sound

Although most children with specific language disorders do not have a hearing loss, many of them have not learned to codify environmental sounds. Their ears hear them, but their brain does not perceive them. Even when the children's attention is drawn to specific sounds, such as birdsong, running water, or footsteps, they cannot easily discriminate between these gross sounds when no contextual clue is present. It is even harder for them to distinguish between musical notes played on the same instrument, and harder still to sing these notes.

Visual and kinaesthetic aids are used in the teaching of the auditory skills needed for the understanding and use of spoken language. For the same reason, and in a similar way, they are also used in musical context. We must teach children to discriminate between short and long notes, and between pulses, that is, between triple time, quadruple time, and, the hardest, duple time. They must learn that notes of different lengths are permitted to make different rhythmic patterns: and that these notes are pitched at different levels. It may also be possible to introduce the existence of the further differences of musical expression; speed, intensity, and quality. But these must remain constant until such differences are being specifically introduced. And perhaps the concept of harmony may be added later. This kind of information needs to be presented in the right order, which seems to be: duration, pulse, rhythm, pitch – that is, the elements of melody; and then the more subtle distinctions of dynamics and harmony.

Rhythm

It is important that a child's ability to beat in time to an even rhythm should be judged only in relation to the pace he sets for himself, which is usually faster than that of an adult. Teachers have been known to report that a child's rhythm is poor just because he cannot conform to their adult pace. This is unfair to the child, as this task may be just as difficult for him as it is for an adult to skip to piano music which is being played at a pace suitable for children. Perception of the regular accent at the beginning of each bar, showing the time of the melody, is important. Its phrasing, shown by the grouping of bars, and a slightly heavier accent on the first member of the group, is less important at this stage.

Pitch

The 'falling third' interval, for example G to E, occurs naturally in the play of most young children. It therefore seems sensible to introduce the concept of pitch with this interval. But language disordered children need a wider one, a fifth. It is more important to make children aware of intervals than of the pitch of single notes. Dr Ronald Senator, in a personal communication, writes:

> Typically natural intervals, like the falling third, or the rising fourth, or the falling fourth, all occur in language inflections all over the world. They are universal structural pillars in traditional musics because they correspond to perceptive and neurological processes of

sound cognition. For handicapped children, one is then appealing to mental functions which, as many think, may well be innate, with the possibility of aiding disordered functions by directing them. 'Going up and down' is a primary mode of musical cognition and invention, more primary than distinctive pitching. The universality of graphic notations, as in plainchant, is a witness to this. They represent the rise and fall of melody without any attempt at all to pitch exactly. This is the best possible ground to start on, helping disordered children to grasp 'up' or 'down'. This primary shaping of a tune is a fundamental training for all children.

It is possible to illustrate 'low' and 'high' notes with three children standing: one on the floor, one on a chair, and another on a table. These heights are associated with pitch patterns such as 'low, higher, highest' and 'high, lower, lowest'.

Other methods of illustrating pitch are simple laddering; mathematical structural rods (see p. 116); and the seven Kodaly hand-signs, each corresponding to a note in the sol-fa. The possible disadvantage that these may become confused with Paget signs is theoretical only; in practice the children realize that these are part of a different system, in the same way as they recognize the differences between the various educational uses of colour.

Musicolour

This is proving to be a successful method of teaching basic awareness of rhythm and pitch to language disordered children. It has been adapted from the method devised by Dr Ronald Senator, and described by him in a booklet of the same title. He states that it 'has been invented to portray to the eye the workings of musical operations by which all music is formed; and in a way simple and direct enough for a child to grasp, without the need for complex technical language.' The adaptation has been made by Margaret Campkin, from whose booklet the essential elements are extracted.

Ronald Senator's method highlights a correspondence between the languages of mathematics and of music. He produced a set of coloured rods, similar to Cuisenaire or Colour Factor, as visual and tactile aids to teaching the theory of rhythm and pitch. Because of the similarity between mathematics and music, it is essential to use the same colours for both. During the experimental period, the mathematics rods were used, but were found to be too small to manipulate as quickly as was necessary in music teaching. So a new set of rods with corresponding colours and in a larger size was made specifically for Musicolour. Now the children's understanding of both mathematics and music cannot fail to be enhanced by the implicit connection between them.

The materials of Musicolour comprise eight strips or rods of proportional length of different colours. They are used horizontally to represent lengths of time, and vertically to indicate intervals of pitch. They are shown to the children by the teacher, and later selected by the children to show whether or not they have understood what they represent. They are enthusiastic about handling the apparatus, because they see the activity as fun, so motivation and concentration present few problems. Their memory improves as they become able to work with increasingly longer series of visual patterns.

Simple tests have been devised as a means of assigning children to homogeneous small groups. These tests assess rhythmic awareness. Each group then meets weekly, for about 15 minutes. More than one weekly session would be preferable, but time-tabling limitations usually prevent this.

Auditory discrimination

First, the meaning of the words 'same' and 'different' is transferred from the visual to the auditory modality, by asking the children to listen to three non-pitched percussion instruments; for example, a drum, maracas, and a wooden block. The teacher tells the children whether she will play the same one twice, or two different ones. But then she asks them to listen and to tell her whether she has played the same instrument or different ones. So far, they watch as they listen. But later she plays the instruments behind the children's backs, or asks them to shut their eyes before she plays, and to keep them shut while they are listening. This sequence routine is retained in more advanced listening tasks.

Rhythm

Success in this discrimination task is essential before the teacher can proceed to the more difficult rhythmic one. A simple rhythmic pattern is played on one instrument, and a second one follows, on the same instrument. It is either the same or different. It is at this stage that Musicolour rods can begin to serve as visual, static, aids.

A set of Musicolour rods for each child comprises a specially made stepped tray, which holds eight rods, cut from lengths of wood two centimetres square. Although the colours correspond to those being used in mathematics teaching, there is one exception; the eighth rod must be the same colour as the smallest. The teacher also has 50 each of the five smallest rods.

A series of small cards is also needed. On each of these is drawn either a four-rod, or a three-rod, or a two-rod, or a single rod. They should be seriated, so that the child can tell at a glance the number of beats each one represents.

The teacher plays one, two, three or four beats, and the children respond by selecting the corresponding card each time. When every child has collected one of each card, he picks up the appropriate one as the teacher plays or claps its rhythm. Then the children play or clap the rhythm of a card indicated by the teacher. Later, each child plays, one after the other, the same rhythm on a different instrument, so the sequences are repeated to make longer rhythmic phrases. Permutations on this theme continue to increase awareness. Children's names are clapped, and sorted into groups according to the number of beats, or syllables, they contain. Familiar words are classified in the same way, and short sentences are included in the three- and four-beat sections. Throughout these activities single one-beat rods are often matched to the cards, and vice versa.

When the children can confidently match one-beat rods and cards with each other, the two-beat rod is introduced. This represents a long sound in comparison to the short sounds of the one-beat sequences. Long sounds are most easily produced by the teacher's voice or a recorder. They are combined with short ones, so rhythms containing series of mixed long and short notes can be played, recognized, represented by cards and rods, and finally sung, clapped, and played by the children. Rhythmic training can be reinforced by walking, using short steps and strides to indicate the difference between short and long notes. More children's names can now be assigned to specific patterns. And the rhythm of simple four-phrase tunes can be taught by cards, rods, or a wall-chart showing the rhythm of each line.

Pitch

Awareness of pitch is approached in a similar way. It is for this purpose that the eighth rod must be the same colour as the smallest, to represent the same note 'doh' at different levels. But the first musical interval to be introduced must use two different notes. And, because language disordered children need to distinguish between greater differences before smaller ones, the doh-soh interval is the most suitable one to choose. The teacher sings it in one of the keys from C to E inclusive. The interval at this pitch level can be encompassed, eventually, by the singing voice of all the children, being not much wider than the range of a normal speaking voice.

Now the rods are re-introduced, to be used in a different way. The smallest one represents 'doh', and the fifth one 'soh'. Here the Kodaly hand signs for the eight notes in an octave may be introduced as an additional visual aid. Children learn to associate, more and more rapidly, the notes, rods, colours and hand-signs with each other. Any of the four representations can be used by the teacher as a stimulus for the children's response, which can be shown in any of the other three ways. Later, each child takes a turn of assuming the teacher's role. Thus they all have an opportunity of judging the accuracy of their peers' responses, which increases their auditory discrimination skills still further. Names can be sung to different sequences of dohs and sohs.

The note 'me' can be introduced, by the third rod, much more quickly, as, once the matching concept is grasped, it can be extended with less explanation and established with less practice.

Plate 11.1   Musicolour rods are being used to teach pitch awareness.

Chime-bars, labelled appropriately with 'doh', 'me', 'soh', can be assigned to three children who play satisfying tunes in response to the teacher or another child conducting them. They learn to sing the notes of these tunes, and, later to add simple words to them.

'Re' and 'fa' join the first three notes, and more complex note-series are attempted. When the children are able to attend to both rhythm and pitch visual aids simultaneously, the rhythm rods can be shown under the pitch rods in an array on a flat horizontal surface, or on a wall-chart.

The majority of six- and seven-year-old children with severe language disorders cannot sing in tune. But after a two-year Musicolour course amidst other less specific musical activities, most of them improve. This is only one of the positive results of such training. It cannot fail to improve, to some degree, the skills of auditory perception, discrimination and memory, and in turn the language skills which rely on the appropriate use of these.

Singing

The singing of short musical phrases for reinforcing basic understanding of rhythm and pitch is included in the systematic approach of Musicolour.

But the singing of short and easy songs cannot be postponed until a certain level of understanding is reached. In particular it is advisable to avoid all nursery rhymes. Young children with language disorders should not be confronted with what is to them irrelevant vocabulary, inverted syntax, and semantic nonsense. Occasionally a 'real' song can be attempted. But the teacher's choice is limited to those which satisfy as many as possible of a number of criteria: the familiarity of the concept, linguistic structure, and vocabulary to the children; the simplicity of pulse, rhythm, intervals, and pitch-range; and a minimum number of musical phrases to be remembered.

Before these real songs are introduced, it is wise to teach simple songs which have been specifically written or adapted, to suit the necessary criteria. If the rhythm and pitch cannot be easily demonstrated with Musicolour rods, it is likely that they are too difficult. Each one, at its point of introduction, should be relevant to a concept currently being studied by the class. Familiar words should be used, and these should be strung together in a form as near as possible to the syntax which can be understood by most children in the class. Linguistic inversion should be avoided.

The melody is played on the piano, with no harmony at all, or a very simple one, possibly with chords strengthening the accented notes only. The children listen several times, and then join in by clapping the rhythm.

Then a visual aid is produced. Some songs can be illustrated with pictures alone, but most need a few written words. Each one is written on the blackboard, or on a large sheet of card. The teacher points at the words

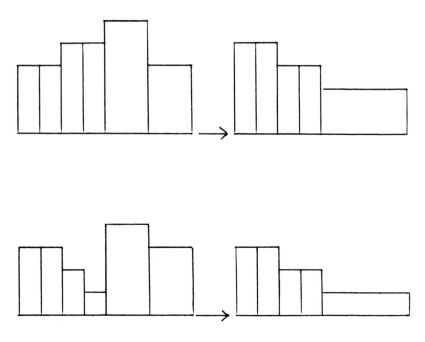

Figure 11.1   Musicolour pitch-pattern of a simple tune

as she reads them aloud. After a few repetitions the children join in. When they have grasped the global meaning of the song, the teacher reads and points rhythmically, to correspond with the tune. Then, as she plays the melody again, the children read the words rhythmically. When this can be achieved, they are invited to sing the tune. If tune and text together prove too difficult, one word can be selected, and the whole tune sung to that. This can be repeated with as many words, or as many times, as necessary. Or, the tune can be hummed.

There are several possible variations on this method. The words of the song can be displayed within a 'staircase' which is stepped in size and direction according to the pitch line. Or, more clearly still, they can be written below a Musicolour pitch pattern drawn out on squared paper. It is usually too confusing to add the rhythm pattern separately, but this is implied in the horizontal length of the drawings of the pitch rods.
The use of this method is most satisfactory with tunes comprising mainly one-beat notes.

Indications of intervals can be given by Kodaly hand-signs or by simple laddering, which is easier for the teacher. Imagining a ladder between her and the children, one of her hands shows movement up and down the ladder throughout the tune.

At first simple tunes can be quickly composed. The most suitable words are those with which the children are already familiar, such as their own names; and then common phrases like 'fish and chips', or 'put it away'. Later others can be selected for their simplicity, or because they are well known to most people. This is one of the ways in which the children can be introduced to the tunes commonly enjoyed because they are part of the nation's musical culture. It is difficult to make generalizations about such tunes. Their quality defies description. Words can be sung to those which are normally played instrumentally. Or, the words of well-known songs can be sung to those which are normally played instrumentally. Or, the words of well-known songs can be replaced by an entirely new set of words, such as:

> 'Where do you live?' } sung three times, with his own home town
> 'I live in Shoreham' } inserted by each child,
> 'All of us live in England'.

The tune is 'John Peel'.

Original words of other songs can be slightly altered, so that the basic meaning remains, but the way in which it is expressed is more suitable for language disordered children. This applies particularly to hymns, and especially to Christmas carols.

The voice can be produced more clearly if for a minute or two a pencil is held harmonica-fashion between the front teeth while the child is speaking. He automatically continues during the next few minutes to produce a more powerful tone. If that is while he is singing, the result is far more confident.

When movement is allied to music, there is no doubt that they are mutually useful. The Dalcroze method of teaching rhythm and pitch is applicable in this context. And Margaret Morris Movement's systematic approach (described in chapter 10) provides not only movement, but also the opportunity for the improvement of rhythmic skill.

During their first years at school, language disordered children have a lot to learn. They must be taught basic language skills, and there is no time to waste. But music is a vital part of the curriculum, and should not be relegated to time-table slots where the children's concentration is at its lowest. It has many purposes, some basically linguistic. But it also lays a foundation for musical activities to be undertaken later in life. It can lead to music-making, which is pursued for its own sake, both by individuals and by groups. Exploration of sound is important, so is a basic understanding; and both of these lead to increased enjoyment of the art itself.

12 Helping thinking? . . .

At least half of every school week is spent on very specific language activities. These include the mechanics of handwriting and spelling, writing and reading. All of these activities are based on the synthesis and analysis of the different levels of the English language itself, and the associations which must be made within and between those levels. Not only are they approached by structured methods, but their content too is the structured grammatical aspect of the language. It is also important that all written and spoken work produced is related meaningfully to the real world, and that children are encouraged to use speech and writing appropriately in spontaneous communication.

Few, if any, of the activities covered during the other half of the timetable do not include some aspect of language teaching. The children must become aware of their own environment, and learn to make correct associations between their experiences. How does any child with normally developing language ability learn that chips are made with potatoes, and not caught like fish? or that the green circular slices called cucumber are cut from the long green object bought from the greengrocer which has the same name? There was a time in all our lives when we did not understand these concepts; and because we do now, we must have gradually become aware of them. It may generally be thought that most children learn this kind of association when they are very young, for example, while playing in the kitchen as their mother is preparing meals. They may be given the tools with which to help in this transformation process. Most language disordered children have shared experiences with their normal siblings and friends, but they have not learned to understand the relationships between raw materials, the processes carried out with them, and the results. The language problem is often the tip of the iceberg of a disorder which permeates the children's fragmentary knowledge of how the parts of their world fit together, and it inhibits all learning.

There is sometimes a comparable delay in the understanding of children whose primary problem is a visual handicap or a hearing loss: but the degree of delay in a child with a severe specific language disorder can be much greater. When a seven-year-old child denies the association between the parts and wholes of potatoes and cucumbers, one wonders how he tolerates the confusion in his mind about his other experiences which are probably less important to him, and therefore less salient, than food. Is it surprising that some children employ defence mechanisms, which can be confused with autistic tendencies, to counteract the effects of this bewilderment?

Early concepts

A list of the most frequent nouns in the vocabulary of a normal six-year-old child is an essential guide to the development of concepts and thence to the choice of material for children entering a 'language class'. In this context this vocabulary itself is not as important as the concepts with which the words are associated, and related concepts of actions, attributes, positions, and those which defy simple categorization.

Imagine a young language-disordered child in his own egocentric world. There are people and things around him, which he sees, hears, smells, tastes, touches, and possesses. He may have feelings about them, and he may think about them. But his perceptions are uncoordinated: to him each item is separate, as his thinking is not as organized as that of his normal peers. This disorganization is not immediately apparent. It may become more apparent gradually, as the child learns to use language. The adults around him are surprised at his misconceptions, and are faced with a task which, because of improvement in communication, may increase in complexity. They must try to put themselves in his place, to see things as he sees them, and then to present to him facts about his world which are organized in a logical way. As he begins to understand simple relationships, he builds up a set of coordinates which he learns to use in other situations. If eggs can be boiled, poached, fried, scrambled, while still retaining their egg-ness, then perhaps potatoes appear in different forms, and beans, and cucumbers. . . .

At first, very frequent vocabulary is generalized, such as 'man' and 'coat'. It is important to make local decisions about a common word to describe a class of clothes like pullovers, jerseys, sweaters, tops, jumpers, and any other similar garments. Children who learn words slowly must be taught only one word which can be used for any of these items. In the early stages the children must be given the minimum number of words to describe the maximum number of things. Later, distinguishing differences can be pointed out, and the necessary vocabulary added.

Early conceptual associations

An increase in noun-vocabulary may lead to a greater accuracy in communication, but this makes very little contribution to the development of thinking skills. People must be associated with appropriate actions, described by verbs; and the verbs with appropriate things, positions, and tools. Verbs and their actions relate animate subjects and inanimate objects with each other, and, in the same way as the nouns, must be generalized. 'Sitting' must be understood to be 'sitting', whether the subject is a woman, a boy, or a cat; and whether the subject is sitting on a chair, a park-seat, a stool, or the floor. 'Eating' must be known to be 'eating' whether the subject is a person using cutlery, or a dog using none.

Next in importance, and even more difficult to generalize, are attributes of people and things. Is the girl happy? or not? Is the sock wet? or dry? What things in the room are red? or hard? These qualitative words are precursors to the more complex concepts of shape, number and measurement, including that of time, and must be grasped before more advanced ones are approached.

Further essential concepts are those of position: the demonstrable meanings of 'in', 'on', and 'under' must precede the more idiomatic ones. 'In the cup', 'in the sink', 'in the box' can be perceived more easily than 'in the road', or 'in the sun'. 'On the table' is easier than 'on the wall', 'on the bus', or 'on Friday'. Others, for example, 'across' and 'through' are harder, and 'between' more difficult still. Manual signs, especially Paget–Gorman, ease the burden.

Until simple concepts which can be tested by the questions 'who?', 'what?', 'what . . . doing?', 'what colour?', 'what . . . like?', and 'where?' are thoroughly understood, there is little point in proceeding to concepts of time, manner and causality. Although some language disordered children can give learned answers to some types of questions before they really understand them, this type of activity is misleading and useless, and can even be counter-productive.

Still more complex, and still more difficult for language disordered children to learn, are those concepts for which closed-class words are used, such as 'every', 'still', 'just', and 'only'. These are the ones which all adults concerned with language disordered children should make a conscious effort to include, alongside and throughout the teaching of factual information about the real world which is easier for teachers to present.

The structure of content

It is just as important to organize the content of a series of environmental lessons as it is for a logical grammatical sequence. Although a nine-year-old child in a primary school has usually covered a wide variety of topics, a child with a severe language disorder enters school with much less background information than that assimilated by a normal child in his first six or seven years. An effort must be made to organize a child's experiences in such a way that he consolidates the minimal information that he already has, and gradually finds new ways of gaining more. He must learn how to learn. A teacher's general aim in the selection of concepts must be to make haste slowly. Much time has been lost: some of it must be reclaimed, in order to encourage a later acceleration of factual learning.

Children with language disorders must be shown ways of understanding their immediate environment. We may call them environmental studies, or projects, or even geography, history, and nature study or science. Some take place in the classroom, while others comprise short simple visits, each with a single aim, to places in the near vicinity of the school. All irrelevant incidents must be positively disregarded.

A visit to the kitchen builds on the common previous experience of food. Watching the cook leads to discussion about the meals that are being produced, together with learning the names of utensils and the words describing the cook's use of them. The children watch carrots being cut up; flour, margarine and eggs being mixed; and puddings being stirred. On returning to their classroom they mime, or model, or draw what they have seen. If they can write a few words they label their work: and those who can write sentences record 'The woman is mixing the eggs with the flour' or 'I am cutting the carrot'. It is important that children should not usually use grammatical structures which are more advanced than those they are writing in a language lesson. But the teacher must ensure that in this context it is the concept which takes precedence over syntactic constraints.

Some of these children have an obsessive nature which prevents them from agreeing to changing the type of clothes they wear as the seasons change. Simple discussion about the relationship between thickness of clothing and temperature is necessary. This can be recorded too.

'It was cold. I was wearing a thick jumper.'
'It is hot. I am wearing a thin shirt'.

A simple study of furniture and rooms helps a child to make sense of his own house, or residential school, and the activities for which each room is designed.

'We were sitting on the chairs.
We were sitting by the table.
We were sitting in the dining-room.
We were eating the dinner.'

and

'I was sleeping in my bed.
I was sleeping in my bedroom.
Jack was sleeping in his bed.
He was sleeping in his bedroom.'

Appropriate drawings illustrate each set of sentences. Or classroom room-models are made, pipe-cleaner people sit, sleep, and work. If colour-coding is used to distinguish word classes in syntax teaching, the models are labelled with orange noun-cards. Another day the same models are labelled with yellow verb-cards.

Quick-growing seeds and plants in the school garden or the classroom are a good preparation for visiting the local greengrocer's shop. This is a logical introduction to a longer study of shops in general. A greengrocer's stock matches the scene at home more convincingly than any other. Even a grocer's wares are disguised in packets and tins, and even those with pictures on them are often misleading. People who can read can disregard the picture of a giant on a tin of sweet corn. But non-reading language-disordered children are puzzled by the association even when the tin is opened. This is only one example of incorrect association, which must be avoided whenever possible.

From where, and how, did the greengrocer get his stock? This can be discovered by a visit to a field of cabbages, or potatoes being dug up, or a greenhouse full of tomatoes. If possible most of the tomatoes should be red ones. Some, but not all, could be green, as it is important to point out perceptually accurate examples.

The concept of a simple map is taught within the classroom. Objects on a desk can be moved about, and the positional relationship between them plotted on a piece of paper the same size as the desk top. The procedure is repeated using a smaller piece of paper. The furniture in the room is plotted in the same kind of way. The next step is to draw a very simple map of the relationship between the school buildings and the playground; and then another of the roads nearest the school.

The topic of transport can be approached by watching cars and motor-bikes. 'Where is the man going?' We do not know. But we can guess where he might be going. Local places are differentiated by single facts. Going to one town means a visit to the boating lake. At another there are aeroplanes and boats. A road joins the places together. Buses go along the road. Where are the people on the buses going? Why are they going there?

The construction by each child of his own papier-mâché island is one way of reducing the study of the interrelationship of physical features to manageable proportions. It conforms approximately to a rough shape drawn on a piece of hardboard. It is surrounded by painted water. It may contain hilly ground. The use to which it can be put depends on its contours. Houses, people, farm animals, or an airport may be added. Cardboard roads provide any necessary links between them. Descriptive or imaginative accounts can be written, and perhaps a simple map can be drawn. This activity has the added advantage of laying a practical foundation for the comprehension and following of real maps.

The structure of method

A very specific aim in each lesson is just as important as during a language lesson. Although an environmental lesson is usually given to a class, the individual differences within that class must be considered. The same information is initially discovered by or delivered to all the children together, but rarely just with the spoken word. Any relevant activity must be shared by everyone, as it is important that it must be experienced personally, and not just visually. Dialogue is encouraged all the time. It is advisable to revise the facts to be learnt by presenting them clearly in a visual aid which is built up in front of the children. This demands careful preparation, as it is not easy to do it in an unambiguous way. The choice of vocabulary is crucial, and should be logical, consistent, and as basic as possible. If wine-barrels had been called boxes, no child would have remembered them as wheelbarrows. It is probable that the girl who did this, did not make a sure association between either of these words and the objects they labelled. That they were both containers was incidental. The same child was asked how many buoys she could see. 'There's a boy, there's a boy, and there's a girl', she said as she pointed at the buoys. These incidents took place many years ago before we realized that we were being too ambitious.

When children are asked to make their own individual versions of the visual aid, a teacher discovers misunderstandings, and has the opportunity to put them right at once, with repeated or additional information. And a teacher's judicious questioning about details of children's drawings sometimes uncovers further interesting misconceptions. Not until each child at his own level can explain what he has learned, recording it on the visual aid he has produced himself, can the teacher be sure she has taught what she set out to teach. The process is slow, but worthwhile.

The purposes of any study relating to the real world are many. The language disordered child must be guided to the observation and analysis of relationships between people, things, actions, positions, sources, causes and results which he can experience at first hand. He must be shown how to build his own mental framework with which to think about other environments in which he may find himself later. He must be questioned, not only to ensure his apparent understanding, but also in preparation for the times when he must ask the questions himself. If he has not learned to wonder and to ask questions, he has not begun to learn how to learn.

13 Mathematics

Whatever degree of difficulty is experienced by language-disordered children in the understanding and use of non-number language, that difficulty is magnified as they try to grasp the basic principles of number language. This is not surprising when one considers how long it took early man to conclude that numbers could be generalized to describe groups of different objects; that they did not after all need to use different words for 'five' when they were enumerating five trees, five boats, and five fingers. Some young children with severe specific language disorders do not find it easy to generalize words for people, actions, colours, and positional words. How much more difficult is their perception of the similarity between the five trees, five boats, and five fingers. The fiveness of five is not as simple as it appears to those of us who cannot remember the time when we did not understand this concept.

Yet it is one of the easier ones to grasp. How much more difficult are half, every, enough, heavy, sell, old, yet, and still. These few words represent many more 'number' words which altogether comprise nearly a tenth of the basic vocabulary used in the early education of language disordered children. Their number work does not begin with 'one and one are two'. Their teachers are forced to acknowledge that this is a very advanced concept, which must be approached systematically. When they look more and more thoroughly for any numerical concepts which have been absorbed by the children in their early years, they must not be surprised to find none. Lack of language and communication has prevented the build-up of knowledge and experience from which normal children set out to make their own discoveries, perceive possibilities and experiment meaningfully. The language with which mathematics is taught is itself mathematical. It is not easy to teach the meanings of 'all', 'no' (in the number context), and 'more'. 'Some' is even more difficult, particularly as it so often precedes 'more'. These quantity words, being among those most frequently used by five-year-old children with normal language-learning ability, and others which are used with comparable frequency by this age group, are those chosen as the foundation for early number activities.

There are many other factors which contribute to poor mathematical performance in language disordered children. Mathematical thinking must be even more precise than that required for the production of linguistic sequences. The responsibility for arriving at correct conclusions via a series of logical procedures presents a constant challenge which some language disordered children find daunting. They are rigid and concrete thinkers. They have great difficulty in seeing relationships, making generalizations, and applying principles. They need to work in a narrow area, but at the same time to be encouraged to think flexibly within it. As they become more competent and confident, the area can be expanded. Gradually external direction leads to internal direction. Slowness of perception results in one process being forgotten when another is being learnt. Constant revision is necessary in order to consolidate each stage and link the stages together, to build up a firm basis from which to progress still further. Poor auditory memory is another hindrance. An effective way to overcome this is to record mathematical facts as soon as possible, to reduce anxiety. Written numbers are taught in handwriting lessons before they are needed in mathematical work.

Vocabulary is the foundation of planning

Just as with the other aspects of language teaching, it is important that the mathematical curriculum is based on a basic vocabulary list, ordered as far as possible according to the development of mathematical concepts in any child. So, first all the relevant words must be selected. Early vocabulary is grouped within a grid.

The vertical axis comprises:-

- quantity and/or number;
- size, i.e. capacity and volume,
    area,
    length;
- money
- weight;
- time.

The horizontal axis is based on comparison:-

- between two similar things;
- between several things, which results in various ways of grading;
- between several things, in steps of the same size, that is, *seriation*.

Difficulties in learning about 'number' are complemented by difficulties of a similar degree in teaching it at this level. Most children absorb many basic numerical concepts without any specific teaching. But children with severe disorders of language do not. They have to be taught.

Faced with a vocabulary grid, each teacher must decide whether to teach the concepts in the order of the vertical list, or that of the horizontal lists, or to compromise by choosing a diagonal route of some kind, and if so, what kind. For a linear choice must be made in the early stages. These children cannot learn more than one thing at a time. Initially it is enough for them to tolerate the basic generalizations of quantity or number or

Table 13.1: *Number vocabulary related to quantitative aspects of objects (vertical) and to comparisons within these aspects (horizontal)*

	COMPARISON OF 2 similar things	2 GRADING	3 SERIATION
QUANTITY OF MASS + NUMBER	(a little) _____ all, some, no a lot_____	(bit, piece) more_____ end_____ different, same -er, -est_____ any_____ half_____	part_____ enough_____ middle_____ none
QUANTITY OF NUMBER	1–6 (ORDINAL NO. and GROUPS) next, last_____	every_____ no 1–9 (or 10) (CARDINAL COUNTING) first_____ set_____	every ⎫ ⎧body no ⎬ ⎨one each ⎩thing many_____ 1–20 (NUMBER SYSTEM) both, pair_____ even_____ row
CAPACITY + VOLUME	big, little_____	bigger, biggest more_____	empty full
AREA	big, little_____	bigger, biggest_____ more	small
LENGTH	long_____	longer, longest_____ near, far fat_____ high_____	small thin_____ tall deep metre
WEIGHT			heavy_____
EXCHANGE and VALUE (MONEY)	all, some, no_____ money, penny, pence_____ buy_____	more_____ post	stamp_____ sell_____ save_____ Bank_____

Table 13.1 *continued*

	COMPARISON OF 2 similar things	2 GRADING	3 SERIATION
TIME — simple comparison	all, some no a lot, a little		
	when	early, late	while, until
	long time	race	
	again	yet	ago, still
	now, then	past	soon
	after	before	
	new*, old*		young
		fast	slow
		ever, never	always
— grading	last*, next*	first	once
			often
— seriation			o'clock
— arbitrary units	dinner	tea	breakfast
	clock	watch	
	(day, night)	morning	afternoon
			holiday
— standard units	sun	moon	
	Christmas		Easter
	day		week
	today	yesterday	tomorrow
	night		
	birthday	year	
			Friday, Saturday }
			Sunday
			Summer, Winter

size, without combining such generalizations. They become able to do this only if each concept is introduced on its own.

The number system itself is only part of number understanding and use. Discrimination between small groups must be taught; then the numerals used for representing these groups and for *cardinal counting*; the same numerals are used for *ordinal counting*; and the same again for the more complex concept involving *place value*; and the numbers represented by these numerals must be analysed and synthesized.

Having defined the task, we have sometimes considered omitting number from the curriculum. But who can avoid it in every area of life? One of the most difficult items on our vertical vocabulary axis is money. Even more difficult, and just as important, is time. These two aspects of mathematics are the most common uses of number in the real world. And they cannot be shelved. Language disordered children grow into adults, who, like all others, must know whether they are being handed the correct change, and how to tell the time and act on the result. Also, language disordered children need to be taught logical thinking, and mathematical reasoning is an important part of this. A linear scheme is difficult to achieve, but not impossible. Neither is a detailed scheme impossible to make. But in practice it is impossible to use. A framework of items to be covered is more realistic. Each child must be considered individually, but not necessarily taught in a one-to-one situation. Class lessons in number are often very productive. Questions at varying levels using the same teaching aids can be directed at different children. They are often interested in each other's questions and answers and sometimes learn from them. It cannot be emphasized too heavily that questioning must be seen as a positive teaching method, not merely for the purposes of testing, but primarily to encourage each child to think. Work in small groups is particularly effective in this context, and teachers must be clear in their own minds which object they have in view. Solitary work should be reduced to a minimum. Squared books with rows of sums, adorned with ticks, or spoiled by crosses, are of limited value in the learning process. Number must be fun and be seen to be fun. But behind this there must be well defined teaching goals. Fortunately language disordered children do not seem to object to hard work. Neither is it necessary to provide complicated teaching aids. The minimum of simple material is preferable to so-called 'attractive' apparatus which can be 'distracting'. One kind of structural rods is essential, but not more than one. Some kind of permanently visible ordinal number sequence is also necessary, and flash card numerals, but not too many. A small amount of real money must be available, a classroom shop which can be quickly and efficiently set out and packed away; and a 'bank' from which the money is obtained, with which to go shopping. Sets of pairs of real objects can be collected into cardboard boxes, for sorting into 'big/little', 'long/short', and 'full/empty'. Handwork materials are useful; and a limited number of sum-cards or number-sheets. Interest is created by the addition of plastic containers and water, 'coat-hanger' scales and 100-gram weights, various time-scale charts, a clock-stamp, and a working clock. No more items than these are essential.

A teacher in a class of young children with language disorders does not have to be a mathematician. But she does have to understand the difference between several groups of concepts which are often confused by many: teaching about numbers one to four or five is different from teaching about numbers five or six to nine; this is different again from 10 to 20, and also from 21 to 99. All aspects of numbers must be taught separately: recognition of groups; cardinal counting, answering the question 'how many?'; ordinal counting, answering 'which one?'; understanding spoken numbers; reading numerals; and writing numerals: when any one aspect is thoroughly grasped, it can never be assumed that any of the others are. The concept of *place-value* is much more complex than most teachers realize. *Grading* is different from, and not as advanced as, *seriation*. Synthesis of numbers is not enough: analysis is just as important. Weight and volume must be seen to be anomalous. Teaching a child to tell the time meaningfully must be preceded by giving him a much wider time concept, and also by teaching something about fractions, counting in fives, and other preliminary sub-skills.

Counting and place-value

There must be a gentle slope of accumulating concepts leading to one of the most important number summits.

Plate 13.1 The cardinal one-to-one association between groups of items and structural mathematical rods is being taught.

Differences

Having ensured the understanding of the basic quantity and number words, 'all', 'some', 'more', and 'no', then the perception of big differences must be practised. At first the differences are so big that it is very easy to see which pile of continuous material like sand has more sand; or which pile of discontinuous objects like wooden bricks of identical size has more bricks. Children are gradually required to make more estimations between random amounts of discontinuous material than continuous material. This defers to a later occasion the eventual necessity of measuring by volume or by weight. and reduces the problem to examples in which the concept of cardinal numbers must be applied. One-to-one relationship is taught as a technique of arriving at a solution to which of two groups has more. By this time differences are small. Perception of difference is still tested only by pointing to one group or the other one. But gradually the question is refined to 'how many more?'. At this stage it is the difference between the groups which is counted, that is, the number which is left over when one-to-one pairs have been made. These quantities can be labelled with numerals, which can be written in colours corresponding to those in the structural apparatus being used. Later, these quantities and numerals and others are grouped, in order to emphasize the similarities between the numerals and the concept of common cardinality.

Cardinal numbers are labels
Having arrived at the concept of number as a new way of labelling, in addition to the naming of objects, and the use of colour words to describe them, any small groups (of two to five) of any discrete real objects can be so labelled. It is very important that the skill of counting is specifically taught here. Experience has shown that most children need practice in a series of stages:

- counting aloud, while moving objects simultaneously;
- counting stationary objects which can be moved if necessary;
- counting groups of similar objects;
- counting objects of varying sizes, avoiding stereotyped presentation at this stage;
- making groups with any of the materials already used;
- sorting pictures such as boats, birds, houses, and people into numerical categories;
- Ludo and similar games can be played when counting of objects is firmly established. It uses yet a different skill, that of using one object to mark steps along a line.

Numbers are sequenced and seriated
Then attention is drawn to the sequence of the numerals. Children are shown that each one represents one more than the previous one.

Counting aloud by rote
Practice can then be given in the instaneous recognition of groups of two, three, and four objects. This inevitably leads to counting, and more than four objects in such a group demand to be counted as they cannot be quickly recognized. This need for counting leads to a desire to learn how to count aloud by rote, that is, without any countable material being present. Some children can do this easily with only a minimum of real understanding. But many children, when they reach 29, have no idea what follows. This is not surprising. A child may suspect that it is 30. But if he then realizes that he has already counted 13, his rote memory may become blocked by the idea all numbers are different, and the one he is about to say is the same as a previous one. What, at this primitive level of understanding, does the difference of a final -n sound make? When the 30, 40 and 50 hurdles are jumped, the numbers from 51 to 99 present less difficulty. But with 44, 66, 77, 88 and 99, children often surprise

themselves, and need reassurance that these numbers do exist. Children must be expected to experience confusion between not only 13 and 30, but also between all the higher -teens and all the higher -tys. The final -n does not seem to correspond logically with the position of the information giving the numeral (3, 4, 5, 6, 7, 8, 9) nor with the mysterious initial 1 and final 0 of the number 10.

Numbers are written

Groups of objects between one and nine can be labelled with conventional numerals. At the same time these should be introduced into handwriting lessons, in which there is less insistence on meaning than on legibility. Most numerals present specific handwriting problems: when a child meets numbers in a handwriting lesson, it relieves him of the necessity of doing two things at once, that is, the writing of numbers and also understanding them, in a number session. Not until he can write all ten numerals, including zero, clearly, should he be asked to write any number beyond 9. There is enough difficulty with these without the additional burden of struggling to produce legible figures. The legibility battle must be won first. He can of course use number labels throughout, so his number education does not need to wait for his handwriting to become easily read.

Place value is introduced

Although it would seem more convenient to teach the numbers 10 and 20 before 21 and 99, it is unwise to attempt it. If it is done, it is probable that children learn the numbers only as labels, in a similar way to their learning of 1 to 9. This not only hinders the learning of the concept of place value, but it militates against it. No number beyond nine can be represented by a single figure. The reason for this must be shown: it would not be possible to invent symbols as far as infinity. The concept of place value is presented in distinct stages, using structural rods, counters or pennies on a small table.

1 They are counted out at one end of the table, into six, seven, eight or nine loose groups of ten. The rest are placed at the other end of the table. Numbers below 60 are excluded at first, because the spoken versions of 20, 30 and 50 do not correlate with the spoken words two, three and five. Although the relationship between 40 and 4 is as clear as that for the -tys higher than 50, it is wiser to delay the introduction of 40, too.

2 The groups of ten are themselves counted, and assigned a written label, selected from the four relevant ones, 6, 7, 8 and 9. The number is written on the left of the card, leaving a space at the right for the addition of the unit figure. The label is placed in the middle of the table.

3 The remainder is counted. The appropriate written label is selected from the relevant ten, from 0 to 9. It is placed on the space at the right of the -ty label. The complete number is spoken. Some, but not all, the children can tolerate the information that seven-tens is shortened to seven-ty.

4 When this activity is thoroughly mastered, preferably in a class-lesson,

the existence of zero, as a place-marker, can be justified, and used.
5 Then the more difficult twenties, thirties and fifties are practised, and
spoken. And lastly the most difficult 16, 17, 18, 19; 15, 14, 13, 12, 11, 10.
Children who have met these numbers before seem very relieved when
their system is explained. Children who are meeting them for the first time
have avoided the seeming confusion. There has been no need until now to
point out to the children the similarity between the spoken –tys and –teens.
And because understanding has preceded this, the problem is more easily
overcome. They can be shown within a 100-square.

The system of place value
Now further counting practice can be given with the visual aid of 100
squares. Children find it very satisfying to gain a mastery over the system
once they have been helped to 'crack' it. The first 100-square is open. The
patterns within it are discussed, and many kinds of games played. Where is
24? Now find 27, by finger tracing along the row, or 64 by tracing down it.
Where is '3' more than '24'? (At a much later stage, where is '3' less than
'24'?). Find 10 more than 24. 20 more. 60 more. Find all the numbers
written with two figures the same. Then study the pattern they make. And
so on.

Then a closed 100 square is used for similar games. They are more
difficult, because, although similar questions are asked, each number is
covered. One number may be uncovered as a question is asked. Children
point to the square which they think provides the right answer, and then
lift its cover to find whether or not they are right.

Figure 13.1   The top left corner of a closed 100-square. The covering cards are
attached with staples.

Numbers have patterns

Miniature 100-squares can be cut from squared paper, enough for about ten for each child. The squares should be large enough for the children to write the numbers easily within them, about 2 cm or 2½ cm. But this is done only by those who complete the main task quickly. This is to count repeatedly the same number of squares and to colour the last one counted each time. Colouring every second square in a 100-square produces parallel vertical lines. Most children, having discovered the beginning of these lines, merely produce them to the bottom of the 100 squares to arrive at the same result as if they have counted their way through, in twos. Some of them apply a similar principle when told to colour in every third square, but before they have proved it. When they are told these parallel lines are not the right pattern for the new number, and the squares numbered 12 and 15 are found for them, they go on to discover the new pattern.

Number is linear

Children learn more about the magnitude of number by making 100-strips. This tests their understanding. So does the task of writing numbers in sequence in columns of anything but 10 or 20 lines. With say 23 on the bottom line, the next number is written beside number one, the 25 beside two and so on. So any clues given by numbers on previous columns have to be searched for, unlike the squares in which the place-value system is obvious. A basic understanding of place value can be grasped fairly quickly if it is taught systematically and carefully.

Numbers are decoded

Decoding practice is necessary, but some children need much less than others. When they hear a spoken number, can they record it in writing? When they see a written number, can they say it?

Which is more?

Understanding the relative value of any two numbers which are not presented within a sequenced array needs to be checked. Which is more, 5 or 9? 13 or 14? 17 or 70? 53 or 35? Experience shows that the concept of 'less' should be deferred. It can cause confusion if introduced here. The better the grasp of 'more', the easier it is to deal with 'less' later.

Numbers also show order

A 100-square is an ordinal representation of both the cardinal and ordinal aspects of number. The 26 toffees in a bag are represented by the same number as that on the house at 26 Park Road. The number of toffees is important, but the same number labels only one house: it happens to be the twenty-sixth house along Park Road. (And even this assumes there are no houses on the opposite side of the road, carrying the odd numbers!). The temptation to label ordinal items, like cloakroom pegs or children's individual lockers, with numbers should be avoided. What is the difference between locker number 3 and locker number 15? Number 15 locker is not five times as big as number 3, nor five times as long, so why does it have a bigger number? If this activity is undertaken, it should be at a stage when most of the children need to be made aware that the same system of representation is used for two entirely different purposes. (The less advanced and more useful alternative is to label pegs and lockers with children's names, each followed by –'s!). It is not necessary to use the final –*th* to show the ordinal quality of some numbers when the concept is first introduced. The most natural situation for using it is when teaching dates. Even when it is used, the easier 6th, 7th . . . 19th should be the first examples given because there is no change to the stems of these words. If the words 'first', 'second', 'third', have already been introduced in some context which was not so obviously a number context, they can take their place in the system at 21st, 22nd, 23rd and 31st, to be followed by their repetition in the first days of the following month. When learning this method of writing dates, children find it simpler to learn the most common –*th* before the three exceptions.

Numbers can be bigger than 100, or even 1,000.
An even more effective way of teaching the place-value concept is to introduce bases smaller than 10. Base 3 seems a slightly easier beginning than Base 2, and just as useful. Coloured structural rods such as Cuisenaire are used, just the ones and threes. We pretend that we know no numbers past three. One-cubes are put out, one at a time, and the increasing number of cubes in recorded on paper. But when a column of three ones has been made, they are replaced by a three-rod. Beside this the same process is repeated twice more. But now we have three threes, so we can make no more columns. The three threes are repeated twice more. Now we have three lots of three lots of three. The whole process so far is repeated twice more. Now there are three lots of three lots of three lots of three. In the base 10 system we would by now have 81 ones; we have their equivalent in 27 threes. And they have been recorded in the following way,

Table 13.2: *Using base 3 to record number 1–81*

1	101	201	1001	1101	1201	2001	2101	2201
2	102	202	1002	1102	1202	2002	2102	2202
10	110	210	1010	1110	1210	2010	2110	2210
11	111	211	1011	1111	1211	2011	2111	2211
12	112	212	1012	1112	1212	2012	2112	2212
20	120	220	1030	1120	1220	2020	2120	2220
21	121	221	1021	1121	1221	2021	2121	2221
22	122	222	1022	1122	1222	2022	2122	2222
100	200	1000	1100	1200	2000	2100	2200	10000

remembering that although we may say three, we have no separate figure with which to record it. We can write only 1, 2 and zero.

A small class or group can continue until either rods or time run out. The place-value system is being practised on a much smaller base than ten, but it is being continued to a number which looks like 10,000 or even higher. To use it there is no need for a child to know anything about 10,000 as such, nor any need for a teacher to say anything at all about 81. That would only confuse matters. Neither is it sensible to try and say the numbers. But the first few could be written in a 3 × 3 '100-square'.

It is well worth repeating the whole process with bases 4, 5, 6, 7, 8, 9 and 10. To see a whole class, after weeks of excitement, breathe a sigh of relief as they reach the real 100, or even the real 1,000, is worth any teacher's personal struggle. Some teachers have learned about bases when they were school children, but there must still be those who have not. Then try it out. . . .

Grading and seriation

The words 'next' and 'last', and the suffixes '-est' and '-er' follow the basic 'more' among vocabulary items which describe the processes of grading and seriation. The frequent 'biggest' leads to the more differentiating 'longest' and 'bigger', and finally to 'longer'. That is, the '-est' of many items is initially more interesting to the child than the '-er' of two items. At a similar stage, the vague phrases 'more money' and 'later' express comparable concepts related to money and time. 'Next' and 'last' are also in frequent use with specific days, weeks, school terms, and years, but mainly by the adults within the environment of the language disordered child. He too may use these words, apparently in appropriate contexts, but with the minimum of real meaning. The words must be taught spatially before their strange and less logical temporal use is emphasized. More than three similar items can be graded as a basis for teaching 'biggest' and 'longest'. The groups are reduced to two for 'bigger' and 'longer'. Then the smallest item should be mentioned. It is 'little' or 'short'. There is no need to use 'small', until later when the comparative and superlative of the smallest item is used. The next is bigger or longer, and the last biggest or longest. It is illogical to teach big/bigger/biggest or long/longer/longest, as it is comparison against items which are not present. Then a longer series of graded items is produced. They are 'little' and 'bigger' and 'bigger' and 'bigger', (or 'short' and 'longer'). Once children can carry out this type of perception and labelling task, they are ready to learn seriation.

Seriation

Seriation can be taught either two-dimensionally or three-dimensionally, but preferably both; and, definitely, actively. It is the basis of all kinds of measurement, and accuracy is essential. Each child needs a large sheet of paper, several long strips of paper, coloured differently from the sheet;

and access to pencil, scissors and paste. The teacher cuts a square off a strip, and asks the child to cut another one the same. He is then asked to cut a shape which is as long as two squares like the first square. He can usually do this. The next task is to cut a shape which is as long as three squares like the first square. A child who immediately puts the two-shape alongside one of the squares on the long strip, and marks the line and cuts along it, is well on the way to learning the concept of seriation. If not, he can be shown how to do this. Some children need only a little encouragement to continue accurately, while others need help more often. But the task is repeated until every child knows how to continue, or until the strip called 'ten' is reached, or until time runs out.

This type of activity must precede any type of linear measurement. Not even linear measurement can be understood until seriation is grasped. And all other measurement is even more difficult. Although the concept of length is approached via those of mass, quantity, volume and area, the measurement of length must precede the measurement of area and volume. Teaching about the value of money can be allied to teaching about length. Weight is much more difficult. And time measurement is the hardest, although unfortunately it is the most useful.

Length and money

Length is the aspect of size from which basic measurement principles can be learnt. It is visual, and primarily linear, although structural rods based on a cube provide examples of the second and third spatial dimensions. Although attention need not be drawn specifically to this, rods teach more than similar two-dimensional material, like the paper strips described earlier. They can be picked up easily and manoeuvred into a variety of relative positions. While any rods whose width is unrelated to their length can be used to teach place value to 99, those based on a cube can be used also when area and cubic capacity or volume are being taught. This is related to the use of small bases to teach place value, and the conceptual circle is complete.

The synthesis of numbers, for example, 3 + 2 = 5, is not a very relevant skill. It is unusual for most people to add quantities, or measurements by volume, area, length, weight, or even time. But it is useful to be able to find any given monetary amount in several different ways, for example,

    20p = 10p + 10p
    20p = 5p + 5p + 10p
    20p = 5p + 5p + 2p + 2p + 2p + 2p + 2p etc.

No-one can distinguish relative values of coins or notes merely by comparing their sizes. But monetary value can be learnt by matching coins with structural rods. The concept of composite units must be specifically taught here, although it has been implied earlier. First the relative length of rods must be studied, and this is done by all kinds of pattern making. What makes 3?, 4?, 5?, 6?, 7?, 8?, 9?, 10?, and later, what makes 20?, 50?, 100?, 500? Children think this is going to be an easy and quick task when they begin it. But they are amazed at the number of different ways in which, for example, five can be constructed. And the higher the number, the more permutations there are. They not only increase, but increase by far more than the children would estimate. It is not necessary for children to record all their discoveries, but when they do, it should be in some seriated form before it is written down as a sum. Then generalizations can be made, as it is shown that, for example: 3 + 1 + 1 and 1 + 3 + 1 and 1 + 1 + 3 can all be constructed with the same rods. The number of permutations is thus reduced to a manageable set.

Five is the first number which can be usefully represented by single cubes, two-rods, and a five-rod, and then matched by coins. This shows in how many different ways a sum of given pence can be paid. Later, ten is made with many permutations of ones, twos, fives and a ten, which again are matched with coins. All other intermediate amounts are made as they are reached. And this skill has to be practised without the clue given by the rods, before it is put to use in a real shopping situation. Children enjoy playing with money. A child with a language disorder cannot tolerate any more steps than necessary between representation and reality, so the money must be real. With random amounts each child can be required to make similar sums. This skill feeds back to a deeper understanding of the meaning of place value. A pound note is not only a hundred ones, but ten tens, by which figures it is represented. Young children's ideas about the sources of money are primitive. And so are those of much older language disordered children. One basic concept of a bank should be introduced. It can be represented by a hundred pennies, arranged in a 100-square grid, from which money is obtained in order to buy items from the classroom shop.

The first experiences of weight

The word 'heavy' is the only weight word which appears among those of high frequency in the five-year-old normal population. Language disordered children have experienced trying and failing to lift full suitcases, younger children, or buckets of water. They know they are 'too heavy' for them. Adults lift the children themselves, and may pronounce them to be 'too heavy'.

Balancing
In the classroom the most appropriate type of scales to introduce first are the 'coat-hanger' variety. One pan holds an amount of sand or plasticine, nuts or shells, and lowers in proportion to the increasing amount being

added. A similar amount of the same material is placed in the other pan, until the two pans are level once more. The same amounts are said to 'balance' each other. A lot of balancing work must precede any lessons on weight. Different substances are balanced with each other. And as soon as possible, before any concept of the correlation of weight with volume can be wrongly assumed, the children must be provided with some very heavy small objects. They must be led towards the discovery that only a few small objects which are heavy, are needed to balance a greater number of bigger, but lighter objects. Until this is realized and expressed as a surprise, it is useless to speak of weighing or to start using conventional weights.

Weight
It is important that, in the early stages of teaching either volume or weight concepts, they must never appear to be interrelated. Conversely, it is also important to re-introduce the balancing of objects whose volume and weight are more proportionate.

Commutation

Another concept essential to the weighing activity is that, if a = b, and b = c, then c must be equal to a. Otherwise no two amounts weighed on the same scales can be known to be equal in weight. This concept must be firmly established before any idea of 'heavier' is introduced in relation to conventional pan scales. As with other pairs of adjectives, the stronger one, 'heavy', must be understood and used appropriately, long before its opposite, 'lighter', is included. This is in line with normal language development. Spring balances, normally used for letters and packages, and in cookery, are not useful until much later. At this stage there is no way of explaining how they work, and the numbers on their faces are too high.

Teaching about time

We live in space, and learn to measure, estimate and record many facts about it. They are full of meaning, as we can see what they represent. But we live through time. We cannot see time itself, but only the recorded facts about it. Young school-age language-disordered children know no more about time than babies. They are not responsible for timing the start of activities in which they take part. They eat and sleep, and play and work, when somebody else arranges that they should do so. Every weekday seems the same to them, and weekends may seem rare: they probably have no idea why the routine of the two weekend days is different from all the others. These children in a residential school who measure time at all, use nights as ordinal counters. After how many nights will they see their families again? Although birthday cards, to the parents of one of these children, measure years, to the child himself the numbers on them are a consistent 'label' for his special day. He may be puzzled to discover that this label does not correspond to the date on the calendar. He knows that on his birthday he is seven, but may not know that he is still seven a few days later. When he has learned to remember the answer to the constant question 'How old are you?'. it is merely a response that seems to satisfy the questioner, and still has no real meaning for him. How can it? It measures something which cannot be perceived visually, and the steps between the number labels are too long. When he realizes that birthdays are labelled serially, and correlate approximately with his vertical growth, another anomaly appears. Why do the heights and ages of his classmates not correlate? It is all very mysterious. Is it any wonder then that learning to tell the time presents such a problem? It is so important that it must be approached gradually, so that when the mechanical skill is finally learnt, it has meaning. Many language disordered children have shown that they do not know two basic facts about clocks: that, if they are working properly, they all show the same time; and that their hands move.

A logical and proven teaching sequence on aspects of time is based on teaching, by visual aids and activities, the fullest possible meaning of:

the days of the week;
morning, afternoon, night, (evening);
today, tomorrow, yesterday;
dates and birthdays;
clocks' relationship to school bells;
time-telling;
weeks in months;
years;
seasons.

Counting on

This is a skill which can usually be assumed by a teacher of children with unimpaired learning ability. But its presence must be proved by every language disordered child, and to most it must be taught. They find it difficult to believe in the constancy of a given number of bricks, counters or sweets. So, given a number of items which has already been counted for them, they are loath to use that number as a basis for counting on. They regard the two groups as one, sometimes even pushing them together, and then proceed to count all the items, starting from one. This must be discouraged.

Computing

Alongside a child's practice in the analysis of numbers by rods and money, he needs to see written numbers and the three symbols which link them in equality and difference: plus, minus, and equal. Simple computing is approached by several means: by linear versions of the 100-square, in which spaces must be filled to complete number sequences; mapping with arrows from one vertical rectangle to another, indicating numbers which are one more, two more, and so on; counting on forwards or backwards, from a given number in ones or in small jumps, or 'skips'; and simple 'sums' presented with either a missing number, in any position, or a missing symbol. These are presented both horizontally and vertically, in order to break through one of the common learning difficulties experienced by a child with a severe language disorder, that of rigidity. For a child who is learning successfully that coloured words (in Remedial Syntax) must be placed in one order, it is even more difficult to learn the opposite concept in number work.

Subtracting

Subtraction is a complex task to any child when he first encounters it; to a language-disordered child it is even more so. It has been found that the 'difference' aspect of subtraction is the easiest to comprehend, and also the most useful. Children do not, in real life, take apples and sweets from each other, and count what is left, but they may be interested in how many more gooseberries they have on their plate, or how many more stars on the chart than their classmate. The subtraction sign is not introduced until the concept is understood, and the subtraction process has been used in order to arrive at a missing number in what looks like and addition sum, such as $5 = 3 + x$. The difference made by the presence of a plus or a minus sign is learned from the sums with a missing sign, described earlier. This is followed by reversed subtraction, that is $5 - x = 3$; and then by a conventional subtraction format accompanied by different questions, such as 'What is the difference between . . . ?', 'how many more is . . . ?' and 'how much change from . . . ?'. The main need in everyday life for subtraction has been reached!

Conclusion

Teaching mathematics to a class of young children with severe language disorders is not easy. But a teacher who realizes its importance, and is prepared to face its challenge, cannot fail to find it interesting and rewarding. It is even more difficult to make generalizations about effective methods in this area of teaching than in any other classroom subject. All that can be claimed is that experience recorded here has been repeated with several classes over a period of many years. It is offered as a possible solution to the problems of other similar groups of children, or as a basis for modifications which could prove to be even more successful.

14 Concluding . . .

The age range of the children in the John Horniman School is five to nine years. In 1958, when the school opened, it was considered that by the time they were nine they would be ready to return to normal schools. About a quarter were placed at Moor House School, which had been opened for language disordered children in 1946, and which provided for children up to the age of 16. Others went to schools for the hearing-impaired, or for the maladjusted, or for those with low intelligence. In 1965-66 a follow-up study of 49 children was carried out. It was found that, 'of the 26 children who had been recommended for ordinary school on leaving, at the time of the survey, seven were receiving remedial teaching and only 19 remained in ordinary schools. Two of these children were two to four years backward, and a further 12 were in low streams or reported to be in difficulties. Only five were maintaining satisfactory progress.' It was considered 'possible that the earlier difficulties, although now resolved at a symptomatic level, were a continuing disability. . . . The educational difficulties may not be only secondary to the speech and language disorder but both may be symptoms of a pervasive handicap for which ordinary school placement is unsuitable' (Pauline Griffiths, 1969).

A few years later another ICAA school, Dawn House School, was opened, for children up to the age of 13. However, it was found that children at that age were still not ready for mainstream education. It was then realized that the children with severe specific speech and language disorders needed specialized help, both by speech therapists and teachers, during the whole of their school lives, and possibly thereafter.

At the other end of the age-group, a Day Unit for a class of three- and four-year old local children was opened at John Horniman School in 1976, by the Invalid Children's Aid Association and the West Sussex Education Authority. The children come every morning from a comparatively small catchment area, within a ten-mile semi-circle to the west, north and east of the school. The language impairment of most of them is not as gross as that of the children in the main school. The programme is modelled on the experience described by Cooper, Moodley and Reynell (1978) in *'Helping Language Development'*. Some elements of the Derbyshire Language Programme have also been introduced. It is considered that another of the main factors contributing to the success of the children in the Unit is the consistent use of Paget–Gorman Signed Speech, which demands their attention, and gives a basic order both to concepts and words.

All indications are that the sooner the remediation is begun, the more effective it is. Structure for the under-fives works just as well as for the rest

142

of the age-range. It is a practical proposition from the age of diagnosis. Full cooperation from parents enhances success. Classes from the age of three have made it possible for most children to enter mainstream education at five. They manage to continue to learn alongside their peers, despite some residual difficulties. Thus it is possible to avoid years of disappointment and anxiety both for the children and their parents.

Although in this book an attempt has been made to include as many details as possible about the content of an appropriate curriculum, and about some effective teaching methods, these cannot be implemented unless someone is allocated a realistic amount of time to construct a practical school timetable. Although it is based on class groups, some language activities require smaller groups. So positive cooperation between speech therapists and teachers is essential. Each must inform the other about broad and specific aims for individual children, and this kind of information needs regular updating, if even occasional minor clashes of demands on the children are to be avoided. Speech therapists work mainly with individual children or small groups, either in another room or within the classroom. Teachers work mainly in the classroom, with the whole class, or with small groups, or with single children. All the time their teaching is based on each child's individual needs. Teachers need to keep daily detailed attainment records. They must not be complicated, but simple enough for a substitute teacher to follow in the event of the regular teacher's absence. These records take time to organize, but, like an effective machine, save not only time but nervous energy, in an environment which should be as orderly as possible. These children learn best from a teacher whose demands are made calmly, in an uncluttered classroom.

A balance has to be struck between too little professional specialization, and every remediator using her own expertise to its greatest advantage. Teachers acquire gradually the varied skills and knowledge of systems which they need to use, most of which are very different from those in use in normal schools.

This book provides only one curriculum framework which has been found to be effective. Any such scheme used with these children must take into account the potential problems which will probably be encountered in every class, that is:

- general immaturity;
- social unawareness;
- inattention;
- poor concentration;
- slow reactions;
- poor perception of what their ears hear and their eyes see, that is, poor comprehension of the world about them;
- limited representational ability;
- faulty associations between:
  concepts and concepts

concepts and symbols
symbols and symbols;
- poor sequencing skills;
- poor memory, short-term and long-term;
- difficulties with motor coordination, gross and fine;
- rigid literal thinking;
- immature reasoning ability;
- poor comprehension of language;
- limited reading skills;
- limited expression about events;
- unintelligible or poor speech.

A further quotation from the former headteacher at John Horniman School summarizes the paradoxical situation facing the teacher of language disordered children:

> The common objections to structure are well known – that it leads from rigid, stereotyped thinking to a rigid, stereotyped performance and the assumption is that education in the true sense will never take place. This is a very real danger, but only if the teacher is also a rigid, stereotyped thinker. The successful teacher of language disordered children has to change her attitudes fairly drastically. Her function in the early stages is almost totally directive, and she is imposing systems on children which should have developed naturally. She is concerned less with children's interests and more with children's needs. That is not to say the children's interests are totally disregarded. Their experience and the gradual extension of this is fundamental in planning the programme, but the priority with the young children is filling the linguistic and conceptual gaps, so that they comprehend and appreciate their immediate environment, and aren't allowed or led by the teacher to go off at tangents, interesting though these may appear, and extend the frame of reference too far for understanding.

It follows that a teacher of young language disordered children cannot be expected to teach successfully unless she is allocated a frequent, regular and undisturbed hour or two for thought, which includes planned and purposeful discussion with her co-remediator, the speech therapist.

One book cannot provide a complete prescription. There is an increasing body of theory which awaits being turned to practical use – on attention, movement, comprehension, memory, thinking, and the use of language. There is no conclusion. There is only progress. . . .

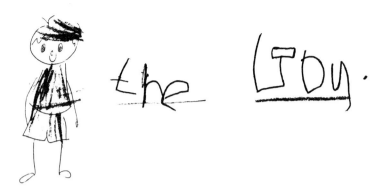

the LʒDY.

First sample of Roger's written work, during his first term at John Horniman School. (The teacher drew the picture.)

balls by the tree. The
balls are for chilren to
play with the balls. The
boy and the dog are
in the boat The ducRs
are swimming in the river.
The river was blue. The cows
are eating the grass. here
are lots of trees. The
trees are green. mummy
Daddy and the baby and

Second sample of Roger's written work, during his last term at John Horniman School, using his word-folder.

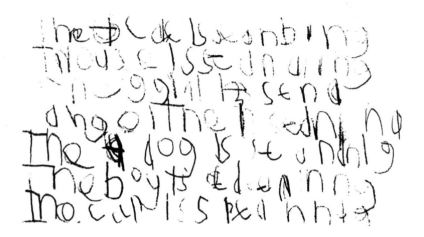

First sample of Edward's written work, using his word-folder, during his first term at John Horniman School

The boy is by the bed.
The is Helen the cat.
The ball is big and gn (green)
The cat is wt. (white)
The dog is st. (sitting) The bed
is red. Mummy is wr. (working)
Nigel is eat the orange
Kelly is playing wrall (with)

Second sample of Edward's written work, done at the same time as his last Report, with no help from word-folder or teacher.

Appendix

REPORTS

The school reports of two children over a period of approximately three years at the John Horniman School are included for those readers who are interested in the realities of the classroom situation. 'Roger' and 'Edward' replace their actual names in order to remind readers that Roger has primarily a Receptive disorder, with an additional hearing loss; and that Edward has primarily an Expressive disorder. Roger's motivation for learning is probably higher than that of most children in the school. Edward's difficulties, despite an average intelligence, normal hearing, and a supportive home situation, are probably greater than most.

Permission for the reproduction of these reports has been granted, not only by Roger's and Edward's parents, but also by their teachers and speech therapists. A change in style reflects not only the decision to alter the report-form, but also, in both examples, a new classroom teacher. And other teachers wrote reports on the subjects they taught. All the report-writers would like it to be noted that these reports were written for the children's parents and their Local Education Authority. Records kept within the classroom are more detailed.

All available reports are included. Term 1 refers to the first term in which the child was at school, and so on. Omissions here are due to those which were made for various reasons, at the time. Both boys were six years old on entry, and between $9\frac{1}{2}$ and 10 years old when they left the school.

Roger

SPOKEN LANGUAGE
(Extracted from speech therapy reports)

Term	Comprehension	Expression
1.	Attention control improving slightly, but still poor. Poor auditory skills significantly affect his level of comprehension. Beginning to understand many PGSS signs.	Has great difficulty in structuring his language. Many omissions and errors in word order. Working on SV-*ing*. Limited ability in the expression of ideas. Spontaneous use of a few PGSS signs.
2.	Attention control improving in one-to-one situation, but	Uses SV-*ing* in structured situations, but not yet spon-

Term	Comprehension	Expression
	still poor in a group. Working on *'Who?'* and *'What . . . doing?'*, but finds them difficult.	taneously. Expressive language is generally tele-grammatic, but he is beginning to initiate a little language himself, with good use of the signs he knows.
3.	Attention control not improving. Poor eye-contact hinders lip-reading. Very dependent on visual clues to help his understanding. Unable to cope well with sudden changes of topic. Auditory recall of only two items.	Beginning to carry learned structures over into spontaneous expression. But most language continues to be telegrammatic, with frequent use of gesture and some signs. Working on possessive -*'s* endings.
4.	Intensive attention training programme is producing good results. Much improved eye-contact. Auditory recall of three items. Shows slightly greater understanding when signs are used with speech.	Working on subject pronouns, and attempting to use them spontaneously. Also working on question forms, *'What is – doing?'* and *'Who is V-ing?'* Language continues to be telegrammatic. But he is gradually incorporating learned structures into spontaneous expression.
5.	Eye-contact still improving. More attentive listening, though still frequently dreamy or distractable. Limited understanding of question forms. Unable to cope with change of pre-sentation in structured work.	Still working on *'Who?'* and *'What . . . doing?'* Not communicating a great deal verbally. Frequently babbles to himself, not initiating communication with others.
6.	Beginning to take greater interest in environment, but finds others' speech hard to understand, particularly when visual clues are weak. In structured situation shows better understanding of question words.	Very good motivation in structured language sessions. Carries $S + is/are + V\text{-}ing$ into spontaneous expressive language. But much of this is still very tele-grammatic. Initiates questions about his environment.
7.	Much more reliable compre-hension of question words.	Learns new structures well, but needs encouragement to

Term	Comprehension	Expression
	Scored at 3.05 year level in Reynell (Verbal Comp.) administered with signs. Now less dreamy, and more inquisitive about his environment.	use them spontaneously. Beginning to pick up many useful phrases from general conversation, and uses them appropriately. Willingness and desire to communicate verbally is increasing dramatically.
8.	Extremely good motivation in all speech and language work. Understanding of questions continues to improve. Can even answer appropriately to questions presented out of context.	Very good progress. Uses a variety of structures spontaneously, using speech and signs simultaneously. Working on *is/are/was/were*, and makes only occasional errors.
9.	More able to think for himself, extracting information that is not clearly stated. Reynell (Verbal Comp.) with signs – age level 4.4 years.	Continues to need practice in use of *is/are/was/were*. Often selects incorrect form. But usually able to correct errors when they are pointed out. Extremely communicative now, even with strangers.
10.	Continues to benefit from the use of signs. Understanding of basic concepts and vocabulary is poor, but is improving slowly.	Able to hold quite lengthy conversations, carrying through and expanding ideas. Continues to make several syntactic errors, but is able to express many interesting and quite complex ideas. Is using his imagination more often.

HANDWRITING

Term	Pencil control	Formation	Spacing	Fluency	General
1.	Poor and immature.	Poor and he can be stubborn.	Poor	—	He is working hard.
2.	Improving.	Improving.	Improving.	Good.	He has worked very hard, and made pleasing progress.
3.	Good.	Good.	Fair.	Good.	The size of letters has decreased, almost too much!
4.	Good.	Usually good.	Good.	Good.	He takes great pains to write neatly.
5.	Good.	Fair, though a little haphazard.	Good when reminded.	Good.	—
6.	Good.	Good.	Good.	Good.	Often careless, but when concentrating his writing is neat. Trying hard with joining.
7.	Good.	Good.	Good.	Good.	Works hard with joined writing, but prefers to do it unjoined. Tends to be careless when not concentrating.
8.	Good.	Good, but it deteriorates with speed.	Good.	Good.	Copies whole paragraphs joined but has not begun to transfer his very good cursive writing from his handwriting books to his other work.
9.	Good, although he still has an immature grasp.	Good.	Good — and uniform depths and heights.	Good, but it deteriorates with speed.	Not so good when concentrating on structures or content.
11.	Making good progress towards remediating his immature grasp.	Good.	Good.	Good.	Continuing to improve.

WRITTEN LANGUAGE

A. Spelling and punctuation

Term

1. —
2. Poor
3. Poor
4. Poor
5. Improved, although still causing problems. He hurries too much to retain spellings.
6. Fair. He finds a phonic approach difficult, especially with his hearing loss, and has to rely on a 'whole word' approach.
7. Improved. His hearing impairment makes the phonic approach difficult. He has been working on capitals and full stops, but does not understand the principles. Does not understand what a sentence is.
8. 3-letter and 4-letter words are learned by a whole-word method. He uses the spellings he has learned in other contexts. Uses full stops, capital letters and possessive apostrophes appropriately.
9. He continues to increase the number of 3- and 4-letter words he can spell. Can also spell many of the long words he meets frequently. He uses the whole-word method, and phonics to a better degree in spelling than he does in reading. Uses full stops, capital letters and apostrophes.
10. He scored 7.5 on the Schonell Phonic Spelling Test. He watches very carefully for visual clues and has some difficulty with words containing sounds that are difficult to lipread, e.g vowel dipthongs and double consonants. However, he has greatly improved. Can now spell over 60 3- and 4-letter words from the vocabulary list. He continues to learn three 4-letter words each week in daily spelling lessons.
11. Schonell Phonic Spelling 7 yrs. 4 mths. at 8 yrs. 8 mths. He added 30 new 3-letter words to his spelling list and is now learning to spell 4-letter words. He has no visual memory problems and retains new words. He has been using a predominantly whole-word/finger-tracing method, although phonic analysis is playing a bigger part. Capable of learning to spell words he sees often. Can now use question marks and speech marks. He often needs to be reminded to use them.
12. Added over 50 new 3- and 4-letter words to his vocabulary this term.
13. Schonell Phonic Spelling 7 yrs. 9 mths. at 9 yrs. 3 mths. Uses phonic analysis to a greater extent than before, although his hearing loss limits him a great deal. Can now spell at least 300 words.

B. Grammatical structure

The following abbreviations are used:

S — subject	D — determiner (e.g. the, my)
V — verb	adj — adjective
O — object	Prep — preposition
N — noun	

Term

1. He is using a folder and colour coding, to help him write about pictures.
   DN   DadjN

2. DN   SV   SVO
   DadjN   PrepDN
   He is working hard and has had little difficulty mastering these structures.

3. DN   SV   SVO
   DadjN   PrepDN
   He continues to work hard.

4. SV   SVO   PrepadjN
   He has been consolidating work on previously learnt structures whilst widening his vocabulary.

5. SVO   adjN   DN   PrepDN
   Plural -s, and possessive -'s.

6. Has been working on the past continuous tense, '*was . . . ing*'. Gradually gaining more than a mechanical understanding of it.

7. Has been working on LTR Two, and revising the past continuous tense, plurals and are/were, and question forms. Occasionally his ideas are in advance of his grammatical ability.

8. Has begun to use question words himself. Has a good understanding of plurals, and appropriate auxiliary verbs *is/are*, *was/were*. Signing is an invaluable source of information to him.

9. Learning to use the simple past tense, '*saw*' and '*went*'. Grasps new grammatical structures very quickly, but signing is an essential means of explanation. His work is predominantly LARSP Stage 3–4 including possessives, plurals, negatives, contractions. Continues to write in the past continuous.

10. Generally LARSP Stage 3 and 4 including simple past tense, irregular past tense, plurals and irregular plurals — future progressive *will be*, *going to*. Coping very well with new work, still using signing as a visual aid. Needs to be encouraged to transfer the learning from this situation to actual everyday conversation, but once he has done this he makes continuous good use of them. Some imaginative writing, including picture sequence cards, story writing, question games, keeping a diary, etc. This serves to reinforce the structures he has learned and to encourage him to use these and increase his vocabulary.

11. Has been working on irregular past tenses. Has been using more complex structures, including irregular plurals and question forms, and possessive pronouns.

12. Has continued to work with irregular past tenses. Has acquired many new verbs. With this new knowledge he has been able to cope with new question form e.g. *'did'*, etc. This in turn has allowed us to teach him the third person singular — gives, takes, brings, etc. Coping very well although he is having some difficulty incorporating this new structure into his spontaneous speech. Needs more work with these question forms also. Has been using adverbs in response to *'how'* questions. Has been introduced to a number of adverbs, i.e. quickly, quietly, etc. Has been working with adverbial phrases using those in different situations, i.e., answering *'how'* questions and using the adverbs to make sentences of his own. Has continued to work on LTR Three and has coped admirably.

13. Has completed his work on irregular past tenses and uses them well spontaneously. Has also been working with *'how'* with reference to adverbs, e.g. "How was the man stroking the cat?" — "Gently". He found the structure quite simple, but needed a lot of work on specific vocabulary. Has also worked on the third person singular, *'he' swims*, *'he' jumps*. Makes errors when he is rushing his work.

C. Free writing

Term

1. —
2. Constructs sentences using a folder of words, colour coding and pictures.
3. Using pictures, colour-coded lines, and colour-coded words, to construct sentences.
4. Constructs sentences with the aid of pictures and colour patterns. Making good use of his word book.
5. —
6. Now writes most of his sentences for his diary, using his word book, to help him with spellings. Uses the sentence-structures he has learnt.
7. Applies his knowledge of grammatical structures to his free writing, and produces good work.
8. Enjoys writing, but tends to write narrative rather than imaginative prose. With prompting transfers the idea he is talking about on to paper. Needs encouragement in order to notice the things about him.
9. When writing totally unaided makes good use of all the structures he has been taught. Free writing is predominantly descriptive,

although gradually becoming more narrative. His improving memory is helping his sequential ability in this area especially.

10. Creative writing is improving alongside his expressive language. Written and oral work are integrated as far as possible to encourage recall and use of vocabulary. Writing becoming a bit more imaginative but he is still writing mainly in the narrative.

11. Has also been writing stories. Has tried to make his stories more imaginative, using questions such as "What might happen next?" "How will he do it?" "What must they do?" "Why?" "When?" etc. Writing stories has encouraged him to use more interesting vocabulary e.g. adverbs, adjectives.

12. This term has been spent encouraging him to think about his free writing. He has been asked to write descriptive and narrative pieces. Has met many new words, and has retained and used them very well.

13. Has been describing things, re-telling stories and events, and has just begun to write his own stories. His written work had been very repetitive, but has become more colourful with more varied vocabulary and structures.

READING

Term

1. Reads back what he has completed in written work. He appears to have a good memory for words. Has been reading DN, e.g. *the boy*; DadjN, e.g. *the little boy*; and SV, e.g. *the boy is running*. Recognizes the names of his classmates.

2. Using early J.H.S. reading material, and reading back the sentences he has constructed in written work. Learning new vocabulary very quickly.

3. Reading early J.H.S. reading material, sentences he has constructed in written work, and parts of his letters from home. Continues to learn vocabulary fairly quickly.

Books	Compre-hension	Phonics	Expres-sion	Fluency	Interest
4. Early JHS material *Ladybird* la *Racing to Read* 1.	Appears good.	—	Reads by signing and speaking simul-taneously.	Good	Good
5. Early JHS material, other early	Appears good at this	—	Poor. Signs and reads	Good	Good

Books	Comprehension	Phonics	Expression	Fluency	Interest
readers, & elementary books.	elementary level.		simultaneously. Speech tends to be a series of grunts.		
6. JHS early readers, *Racing to Read* 1 and 2. Other elementary books.	Appears good at this basic level.	—	Variable. Usually reads by signing and grunting. However with reminders he can produce fairly good speech.	Good	Good. Has a good visual memory for words, and is steadily increasing his reading vocabulary.
7. LTR Two; *Ladybird* books, *Racing to Read*, and other elementary books.	Appears good.	He has some idea of phonics but his impaired hearing causes problems.	He usually reads by signing and speaking, but can read by speaking only.	Good	Good. Likes to converse about the books he is reading, asking questions about the pictures and text.
8. LTR Two *Racing to Read* 3.	LTR books with questions help to concentrate his attention and this improves his comprehension.	Needs the help of finger-spelt letters.	Fair. Improving as he reads story books.	Good	Very pleasing. Enjoys reading aloud. Loves story times and sometimes takes the teacher's place and reads the story.

Books	Compre- hension	Phonics	Expres- sion	Fluency	Interest
9. LTR Two 3a, *Racing to Read* 5. Can read and sign about 600 words in JHS core vocabulary.	Good, especially with LTR Two graded material. Makes good use of pictorial and con- textual clues. A very indepen- dent reader. Grasps new ideas and words with little prompting. Word attack skills are good.	His hear- ing loss affects his phonic discrimi- nation, partic- ularly of conso- nants. Uses initial sounds as a means of identify- ing new words.	Reads well with good intonation. Enjoys reading silently.	Good	Loves to read, and looks upon books as as source of new know- ledge. Chooses books appro- priate to his level of ability.

10. At C.A. 8 yrs. 8 mths. scored 7 yrs. 6 mths. on Schonell Graded Word Recognition Test. He is making good individual progress. He is reaching the final stages of the John Horniman School LTR Two scheme, and has excellent comprehension of this material. Com- prehension not as good with other reading schemes. Finds it diffi- cult to read 'beyond the lines' when confused by tenses, abstract vocabulary, etc. Obviously his hearing loss affects his phonics and he has tended to learn new words by 'look and say', but over the past six months his phonics have improved a great deal, and he is now better able to analyse new words. He enjoys reading very much indeed — and doesn't need any encouragement to go to the bookcase.

11. Can read all 250 words from LTR Two. Has an extensive and varied sight vocabulary. Word analysis is hindered by his hearing loss and he finds phonic discrimination difficult. However he has improved. He is trying to read for meaning and to gain information. Now uses books to supplement topic work. Continues to have a very limited vocabulary and often, although he can read a passage perfectly, he loses all meaning when vocabulary is unfamiliar. Reading has become a way of extending his vocabulary. He is now willing to stop reading to ask "What's that word?" — "Why?" etc., in order to have full understanding of all he has read. He retains and uses

new vocabulary well.

12. Has begun to analyse new words phonically and compare similar sounds in different words. Has an extensive sight vocabulary. Is not satisfied to bark at print, and reads for meaning. His growing interests and ability have led him beyond JHS kernel vocabulary. Has now completed LTR Two and begun LTR Three. Is coping well with the new vocabulary and question forms.

13. At C.A. 9 yrs. 5 mths. scored 8 yrs. 3 mths. on Schonell Graded Word Recognition Test: an excellent result and I feel it is an accurate reflection of his progress. Phonic awareness is growing and he attempts to string sounds together to make whole words. In this test he read words he didn't know or understand, simply by using the sounds of the symbols. The improvement is due particularly to very careful listening and lipreading — he is now reading for meaning rather than simply recognizing the words. He searches for story and information books that he will be able to read with the minimum of help. He now reads and then tells the teacher about it. He has an extensive sight vocabulary.

ART AND HANDWORK

Term	Manual ability	Form	Use of colour	Ideas
1.	Fair	Fair	Good	Good
	Loves art and handwork — likes making patterns.			
2.	Fair	Good	Good	Good
3.	Fair	Good	Good	Good
	Enjoys art and handwork — produces good work.			
4.	Good	Good if a little careless.	Good	Often limited to a yellow house with a red roof.
5.	Good	Careless	Good	Still limited to yellow houses with red roofs.
6.	Good. Most of his drawings are completed at great speed and lack refinement as a result. But sometimes he is careful to put in much detail.	Careless	Good	Good

Term	Manual ability	Form	Use of colour	Ideas
7.	Careless	Good. Drawings tend to be well detailed with many people and objects but very few details on these, e.g. a circle and oblong suffices for a person.	Good	In free drawing still limited to red and yellow houses.
8.	Good	Good. Has now become more interested in detail. Prefers smaller pictures and has more detail in these.	Good	He needs to be given prompts and direction in his art work but once he has been given this he builds on it.
9.	Can use implements and materials without any problems.	Can copy shapes and patterns well. Likes to design intricate patterns. Figures are age-appropriate.	Likes to experiment with colour.	Uses drawings to depict ideas and events.
10.	Has improved in fine motor tasks.	Improving. Thinks before he starts. Pencil drawings show a growing spatial awareness, with more attention given to shape, size and detail.	In design tends to go overboard and often ends up with a blob — This is because he enjoys the mechanics, e.g. splatter paints.	Good
11.	Still improving.	Now including good facial features and clothes in his human forms.	Interested in colour and design.	Likes to use drawings to tell a story, and often divides the paper into sections to draw sequences of events.

Term

12.	Enjoys art and craft, and is capable of very detailed pictures and intricate designs. (He scored $8\frac{1}{2}$ years at 9 years in the Goodenough Draw-a-man test.)

DRAMA

Term

2.	Enthusiastic and imaginative, but can be clumsy in his movements.
13.	Very enthusiastic and works happily in a group. Listens carefully and watches signs closely when instructions are given. Quite imaginative.

MOVEMENT

Term	Margaret Morris Movement	Physical education
1.	Energetic. Starting to learn some of the exercises and develop some control.	Enthusiastic. Works hard. Balancing and co-ordination poor. Team games good.
2.	Attention and control still limited. Some improvement in imitation.	Enthusiastic and lively. Enjoys work on mats, and team games. Poor co-ordination.
3.	Improved balance and imitation and control of movement, but attention still poor. Better response to sound.	Has enjoyed going into the sea.
4.	Attention very poor. When concentrating he is capable of some co-ordination. But overall his performance is quite chaotic. Balance especially poor.	—

Term	Margaret Morris Movement				Physical education
	Footwork	Body Image	Gross Rhythm	Balance and Co-ordination	
5.	Fairly good.	Good	Good	Tries hard, and is improving.	Enjoys P.E., but lacks movement control. Tends to throw himself in the general direction he is aiming at, without any attempt at precision.
6.	Fairly good.	Good	Fairly good.	Works well in some exercises, but deterred by introduction of new ones.	—
7.	Improving	Satisfactory	Quite good	Still lacking in confidence.	—
8.	Fairly good.	Good	Attitude is improving and he tries hard to achieve good results.		Surprisingly apprehensive about climbing, running, etc., but enjoys P.E. Very willing to participate in group activities.
9.	Attention good in one-to-one and group activities. Can be very clumsy, but can imitate position and movement well. Has no major gross motor problems. Able to establish a rhythm, and to innovate quite happily.				
10.	Although he can be clumsy around school, this is due to lack of concentration. In specific lessons such as dance and P.E. he is agile and quick, with good balance and co-ordination. Gross motor skills have improved tremendously in 12 months.				
12.	Aware of rhythm and can imitate and position well in dance. Has good competitive and co-operative spirit in P.E.				
13.	Well motivated and highly competitive.				

MUSIC

Term	Pitch	Rhythm
1.	—	—
2.	—	—
3.	Responsive and attentive. Can discriminate and imitate up to four even beats.	—
4.	Attention tends to wander but when concentrating he joins in group singing by signing and vocalizing simultaneously.	—
5.	When attending he joins in well in singing sessions, signing and vocalizing.	—
6.	Can be quite naughty during group singing sessions, the temptation being great. However, can attend well and enjoys signing and vocalizing to the songs.	—
7.	Joins in group singing sessions by signing and singing. Has to concentrate hard to participate.	—
8.	Is not always eager to join in singing lessons but likes to watch the other children.	—
9.	Enjoys singing lessons.	—
13.	Has a good sense of pitch despite deafness.	Has a good sense of rhythm despite deafness.

MATHEMATICS

Term

1. Counting 1–10. Recognition of and correct reproduction of numerals. Vocabulary — big, little, how many, more, colours. 1:1 correspondence.

2. Pre-number games with structural apparatus.

---

3. Manipulation of structural rods 10s and 1s and a number square 1–100 to gain an elementary idea of place value.
   Recognition of coins and exchanging 2 and 5 pence coins for 2×1 penny and 5×1 penny.
   Addition to 10, adding 1, 2, 3 and 4 to another number without the aid of structural material.

---

4. Recognition of coins, exchanging 1-penny coins for 2, 5 and 10 pence coins.
   Addition to 12, without structural material.
   Elementary work on number bonds. Elementary work on subtraction.
   Good progress.

---

5. Addition to 12 without structural material. Number boards. Subtraction.

---

6. Addition and subtraction.

---

7. Addition and subtraction.
   Time o'clock and minutes, e.g. 10.30
   Recognition and value of coins. Making up values using more than one coin.

---

8. Additions of tens and units — working to 100.
   Money — more or less values; making up amounts using all the coins.
   Change in preparation for subtraction of tens and units.
   Improving all the time. Has a real interest in maths, especially when using real objects, e.g. money. Can see the relevance of number lessons in everyday life.

---

9. Working with tens and units without carrying or decomposition.
   We are working to improve his basic mathematical vocabulary.
   Has been working with '$\frac{1}{2}$' in shape, '$\frac{1}{2}$ past' in time, and amounts of money to £1.
   Has a good understanding of place value and can count using three figures.
   Money — he recognizes all coin values, and his concept of buying power is improving.
   Time — can understand a calendar, tell the time on the hour and half-past, and count in fives around the clock, a skill he uses to estimate and judge lengths of time.
   Size — has a good 'size vocabulary' and can order, match and grade.
   Position — understands the most common position words.

---

10. Computation — has been working on tens and units involving carrying tens. Has a good grasp of place value. Can subtract without decomposition. Adds on, subtracts and makes number

patterns in preparation for multiplication and division without aids but often uses his fingers to help concentration. Time — vast improvement in this area. The work he does in these lessons is integrated with what he is doing in language to help his vocabulary and understanding of tenses. Can read the clock on o'clock, half-past, quarter past and quarter to. Also reading the minutes past, and is being taught minutes to.

Shape and size — has a good grasp of attitudes categories and a growing descriptive vocabulary. Working on $\frac{1}{2}$ and $\frac{1}{4}$ in fractions. Works hard and is coping well.

Money — we use money as a visual aid in computation. He is giving change to reinforce subtraction and adding amounts of money involving carrying.

Weight and length — a long time was spent building up a basic vocabulary in preparation for measuring and weighing. He has now began to use centimetres. Has been working on comparatives, using Paget–Gorman as an extra aid.

11. Has made rapid progress. Brings innovation, creativity and enthusiasm into every lesson. Uses simple multiplication to 5. Has grasped the concept well, after a lot of preparation. Has excellent understanding of place value and can now add tens and units involving carrying. A very independent worker who likes to do project work on his own. Has an extensive mathematical concept vocabulary and is now using standard units in length.

12. Working with multiplication tables to 5. Problem solving has been introduced in order that he may understand the everyday uses and applications as well as the theory of and mechanics of multiplication.

Has continued to work with tens and units requiring the carrying of 10.

Soon I hope to introduce tens and units subtraction with decomposition.

Has also been using centimetres in class and has coped well with measuring tasks.

13. Has been working with multiplication in computation and has a good grasp of the 2 to 7 times tables. Enjoys this type of work and spends half an hour engrossed in it. Has begun preparatory work for decomposition in subtraction of tens and units. Has continued his work on length and can tell the time accurately.

SPOKEN LANGUAGE
(Extracted from speech therapy reports)

Term	Comprehension	Expression
1.	Attention control good for short spells in one-to-one situations. But easily becomes distracted and disheartened by failure. Test results show comprehension up to age-level, except for vocabulary, which is about six months behind.	Mainly single words and 2-word combinations, e.g. *'feed duck'* and *'big man'*. Working on SV. Uses intonation and gesture a lot to get meaning across. Succeeds many times in communicating complex ideas.
2.	Much less distractable.	Uses some LARSP Stage III and IV structures spontaneously, but with many errors and omissions. With Stage II structures he works well and enthusiastically. Still uses gesture and mime, and a few PGSS signs.
3.	Very good. No problems with comprehension. Attends well in one-to-one sessions.	Is making pleasing progress. Working on SV and PrepNoun. Also he is expanding his system in areas not specifically worked on. Good carry-over to spontaneous speech.
4.	Good comprehension. Variable attention. Becomes distracted when set a task which is too difficult.	Excellent progress. Occasionally uses structures up to Stage IV, but with many errors at earlier stages. Working on phrase-level expansions of Stage II and III structures. Makes his needs and interests known despite limitations.
5.	Generally good. But specific difficulties with structures he does not use. Also, understanding of vocabulary still below age level. Attention variable in one-to-one situation.	Works very hard. Makes a real effort to use *'I'* and *'we'* in SVO sentences. His ideas are well in advance of his structures, but he generally manages to get his meaning across.

Term	Comprehension	Expression
6.	—	
7.	Comprehension appears to be good. But formal testing finds specific limitations, particularly in vocabulary. But now more interested in words, and retains them after fewer repetitions. Poor auditory memory. Distractable in group situations.	Making steady progress, but still makes many errors. Can usually express his ideas, and is becoming less frustrated. Uses 4-element sentences, e.g. *Daddy go in car today*. But frequent confusions in word order. In structured language group, working on reinforcement of *'is'* and *'the'*.
8.	—	
9.	Continues to retain new words more easily. Attention generally good, but sometimes stops listening when he has something important to say.	In structured sessions, use of *'the'*, *'is'* and pronouns is improving. But in spontaneous spoken expression meaning takes precedence over structure. Uses coordination, e.g. *'me sitting on it and looking at book.'*
10.	New vocabulary is acquired slowly. He does not understand some structures, i.e., passive; expanded subjects and objects with clauses, embedded relative clauses, and *'neither . . . nor . . .'*.	Difficulty with word-recall still causes some frustration. Uses Stages III and IV structures. *Is/are* are still omitted. Pronoun errors are made, especially in subject position.

Edward

HANDWRITING

Term	Pencil control	Formation	Spacing	Fluency	General
1.	Fairly good.	Unable to form several letters correctly.	—	—	—

Term	Pencil control	Formation	Spacing	Fluency	General
2.	Fairly good.	Letter formations are improving, though there are some reversals.	—	—	—
3.	Fairly good.	Mostly correct. He is very keen to start cursive writing.	Fairly good	Good.	—
4.	Much improved.	Mostly good. He has started cursive writing.	Improved.	Good.	—
5.	Improving.	Good, and getting slightly smaller.	Good.	Good.	—

6. There is little change, since his desire to complete work quickly has meant his concentration on his handwriting has waned. Has improved, though, in more formal handwriting practice.

7. Little change, as his desire for speed leads to errors of formation, and letters missed out. Copying from the board has improved though.

8. Speed still leads to errors.

9. Still erratic, although certain formations have improved, for example, a, d and g.

WRITTEN LANGUAGE (For terms 1–6, see also READING)

Term

2. Can spell own name and nouns.
3. SV, using Remedial Syntax. Can spell three words. Uses capital and full stop.
4. SV, using Remedial Syntax. Can at times produce other structures, but needs help. Can spell several words.
5. SV and VO. Produces new structures, in his letter home for example, but needs help in their final formation.
6 SV, VO and PrepDN. Has good ideas, using a variety of structures, but needs help in sorting them out. Uses his Remedial Syntax

folder. He is learning to spell a few 2- and 3- letter words, using the finger-tracing method.

7. Currently working on the SVC structure. Colour coding is an essential aid to him in structuring his sentences. In a picture-based free writing exercise with the necessary vocabulary available, but no coloured lines, he produced a variety of SV and SVC sentences, some of which were incorrectly structured, most lacked the determiner *'the'*, but there was an occasional full stop. Produces good ideas verbally for his letter home, but needs assistance in the final structuring. Has a spelling vocabulary of about eight words and is currently working on a few two- and three-letter words using the whole word method.

8. See 7.

9. Recent work has been on plurals, adverbial phrases and the SVO structure. The colour coding system is used in teaching these, and he is making slight improvements in structuring his sentences, when this aid is removed. In a typical piece of unaided work he produces good structured sentences in half of the work: in the other half it is clear to see what he is trying to write about the picture, but words are either misplaced or missed out altogether, e.g. *'The cat is table uander'*. Uses a word book in writing his letter home – has the idea, can often find the correct words, but either misplaces or misses words out. He has started some written comprehension work (LTR 2); he is finding reading the question words difficult. Can answer the questions verbally, but when writing the answer tends to miss out parts of the required phrase. In spelling he continues to use the whole-word method, and has a vocabulary of about 21 words.

10. Recent work has been on the SVO and SVA structures, also the use of possessives. Performs well within structure of the colour coding system and is beginning to be more confident in producing his learnt structures without this aid. He is also using his own word book to find the words he needs. One positive step is that he can sometimes see where his omission of a word is, and correct it himself. In a recent free-writing exercise he wrote over 25 sentences describing a picture using his folder and word book. All word order was correct but he used a sentence of six words or more on only five occasions. The majority were four-word sentences such as *'The ball is green'*, or *'The boy is running'*. This shows great improvement but indicates the problems he has in remembering and ordering a longer sentence. His written comprehension work (LTR 2) is improving as he refers more consistently to the text. In spelling he scored an age of 5.7 on the Schonell Test and has a vocabulary of at least 36 words.

READING

Term	Books	Comprehension	Phonics	Expression	Fluency	Interest
1.	Pre-reading materials. A lot of practice is needed.	Recognizes one or two words.	—	—	—	There has been little improvement due to his attitude.
2.	Left-to-right habits are becoming more established.	Knows 10 nouns and 2 verbs.	—	—	—	Quite keen to learn.
3.	LTR One	Very good	—	—	—	Very good
4.	LTR One, and early LTR Two books.	Very good	—	—	—	Very good
5.	LTR One, and early LTR Two books.	Very good	—	—	—	Well motivated. Enjoys reading & listening to stories.
6.	LTR One and Two (Schonell GWRT 5.6 yrs.)	More advanced than his decoding ability will allow.	Limited phonic awareness.	—	—	Wants to read though finds it difficult. Also enjoys listening to stories.

7. Does not find reading easy as he has a poor retention of new vocabulary. However he understands what he reads and is making a good effort. Has a limited phonic knowledge which is being specifically worked on.

9. Test results: Schonell (Revised Norms 1971) — 6 yrs. 9 mths. LTR One vocabulary — recognizes 75 Flashcards. Books — LTR One material; *Ladybird* 2a (revised version); early LTR material, and *Racing to Read* 2. His confidence has improved following some intensive phonic work. He can now give the correct sound

to 18 single written letters. This has helped his analysis of words, particularly the initial sounds. He is understanding what he reads and there is an apparent improvement in the retention of new vocabulary.

10.   LTR One. Vocabulary — recognizes 75 Flashcards. Reading has shown steady improvement, is using his phonic knowledge, i.e., the sounds letters represent, to good effect, particularly with the initial sound. Is more aware when a wild guess is wrong and often makes a more sensible guess or gives the correct word. His comprehension is good and his retention of new vocabulary is steady. Current material includes that associated with LTR One, *Ladybird* 3a (revised version), *Racing to Read* 3, and five LTR Two books.

ART AND HANDWORK

Term	Manual ability	Form	Use of colour	Ideas
1.	Good, as long as the work is free and not directed.	Immature.	Very bold, with very pleasing result.	Good.
2.	Good in undirected work.	Immature.	Bold. Very bright clear work.	Good.
3.	Fairly good.	Immature.	Bold use of strong colours.	Good and positive.
4.	Fairly good.	Immature.	Excellent.	Good and positive.
5.	Fairly good.	Immature. It does not do justice to his ideas.	Good.	Good ideas, supported by good powers of observation.
6.	Enjoys art work.	Immature often due to haste.	Good.	Good ideas, but often not realized in final product. Observes his surroundings well.
7.	Enjoys activities but haste often means being satisfied with	Figurative and pictorial work rather immature.	Uses a variety of colour, and likes to see every bit of the paper	Good.

Term	Manual ability	Form	Use of colour	Ideas
	less than his best.		covered.	
9.	Enjoys these sessions, and is helpful during them. He likes to see the finished product quickly, so often doesn't take his time, which leads to hurried and immature work.			
10.	Does not charge into his work so much. He is aware of his limitations in form, and works within them. He has had more interesting ideas, and uses colour well.			

DRAMA

Term

1. Attention control is usually quite good and he appears to enjoy these lessons. Inclined to be rather silly when working in pairs.
2. Generally, a positive attitude and attention.
   Reticent about trying new activities.
3. Generally works well, but is sometimes reluctant to contribute fully in group work.
4. Shows occasional frustration if he thinks he is unable to do something properly, and then co-operation with peers is poor.
7. More attentive and responsible. Inclined to become a little self-conscious and react to this by being silly in groups and pairs work.
9. Generally, his attention is improving, and can be very good if a particular activity 'fires' his imagination, but he can also be a source of irritation, or irritate his peers.
10. Has become significantly more mature, and attention when listening to instructions and throughout an activity is promising now. Relates more easily to other children and is ceasing to be a source of irritation to them.

MOVEMENT

Margaret Morris Movement

Term	Footwork	Body image	Gross rhythm	Balance	Co-ordination
1.	Good	—	—	—	Fairly good
2.	Good	Satisfactory	Fairly good	Poor	Lacking in confidence

Term	Footwork	Body image	Gross rhythm	Balance	Co-ordination
3.	Good	Good	Fairly good	He rarely makes maximum effort	
4.	Becoming stronger	Good	All improving		
5.	Improving	Good	Attitude is improving, and his movements becoming more controlled.		
6.	Continuing to improve.				

Physical education

Term

1. Works well. Has very well developed ball sense.
2. Good work.
3. Very good ball skills. Timid when trying a new activity.
4. Some difficulty with team games. Bad loser.
5. Inability to accept defeat inhibits full participation in team games.
6. Main improvement is better acceptance of defeat, although still rather immature in this area.
7. Has a good aptitude for ball skills. Much improved team spirit.
9. Generally well-co-ordinated.
10. Well co-ordinated and can do well when he tries. Can be resistant to ideas and needs a lot of encouragement. Much more mature in defeat though unhappy about it.

MUSIC

Term	Pitch	Rhythm
1.	Learning to imitate doh and soh, using handsigns and Musicolour.	Good discrimination of up to 4 even-beat phrases.
2.	Can name and sign doh and soh. Occasionally can sign correct intervals in a tune.	Very poor discrimination and imitation. Only able to imitate one beat consistently.
3.	Knows colour, name and sign for doh/me/soh now. Occasional pitch accuracy, as more aware of intervals recently.	Erratic response.

Term	Pitch	Rhythm
4.	Good consolidation of naming, signing and colour identification for doh/me/soh. Occasional spontaneous pitch accuracy.	Poor.
5.	Working on naming, signing and selecting appropriate Musicolour rods for doh/me/soh combinations. Variable response — usually due to inattention.	Poor discrimination and imitation of short even-beat phrases. More secure with dotted rhythm phrases.
7.	Can name, sign and select the appropriately coloured rod for doh/me/soh. Spontaneous pitch accuracy is variable.	Discrimination and imitation of short even-beat phrases is gradually improving.
9.	Pitch accuracy is showing a little improvement. He is able to name, sign and select the correct Musicolour doh/me/soh.	Continues to find difficulty with discrimination and imitation of short even-beat phrases, but his attention is much better now.
10.	Can name, sign and choose colour for doh to soh inclusive. Often able to sing doh/soh intervals in tune now.	Problems with imitation and discrimination persist.

MATHEMATICS

Term

1. Counting 1–6 alongside signing: 1–1 correspondence 1–5: numerals 1–5: matching numerals to sets: counting to 4 accurately. He has great trouble writing numerals.
2. Counting and signing 1–10: 1–1 correspondence 1–6: numerals 1–6: matching number to sets: can order numbers 1–10 but cannot link this skill to verbal counting or labelling isolated groups.
3. Can add numbers 1–6 to other small numbers: can recognize and write numerals 1–6 well: has done some basic work with money using 1p coins.
4. Can count up to 6, and can read most numerals without any difficulty. His writing is also improved, but he has trouble counting objects, counting in his head without co-ordinating it with the

objects he is picking up in his hands.

5. Confident in counting, matching, recognizing and writing numbers up to 6. Working on 7, 8, 9, 10. His main difficulty is counting objects as he is still not co-ordinating the counting in the head and the movement in his hands with the slightly larger numbers.

6. Developing 1–1 correspondence with numbers above 6. Introduced idea of addition up to 5 using Cuisenaire and other aids.

7. Addition to 6 using structural rods. He is working better alone, but finds number difficult. Using aids successfully though not learning the number bonds involved. Time recognition and insertion of clock hands for hours and half-pasts.

8. Addition to 8. He is working well with structural rods, needing a lot of variety at each stage as he is not learning easily the number bonds, although occasionally surprises us with his knowledge.

9. Addition to 10 using both structural rods and a number line. Has learnt a few bonds, but needs a lot of practice in varying presentations. Is not counting but more confident in working alone.

10. More confident and enjoying the work. He can cope well with addition to 10 and uses his knowledge well with money to 10p. Has learnt some of the bonds and can now use the aid of his fingers. Currently working on the ordering and naming of numbers 10–20.

Glossary of curriculum-related concepts

Cardinal counting answers the question 'how many?', e.g. 4 houses. (See Ordinal counting)

Closed-class words are those in word-classes which cannot be increased, e.g., there are a certain number of pronouns (he, they, everybody, etc.), and no more will ever be needed. (See Open-class words)

Determiner – 'the', and all other words which can substitute for it, e.g. *the* house, *my* house, *those* houses.

Grading – arranging in order of size, e.g. length, volume, value. (See Seriation)

Haptic – the sense by which an object can be recognized by feel alone.

Intransitive verbs normally have no grammatical objects, e.g. 'sitting', but not 'sitting the . . . '. (See Quasi-transitive and Transitive verbs)

Kinaesthetic – in this context, a learning method for the development of word recognition and spelling, in which 'the form of the word is represented by the child's movements' (ref: Fernald, G., 1943)

Modals are a limited set of verbs, e.g. can, must, ought to, which are followed by the stem of a verb, e.g. we should go, I ought to get there.

Open-class words are those in word-classes which can be increased as new things and processes are invented, and new words are used for describing familiar items. Nouns, Verbs, and Adjectives are therefore open-class words.

Ordinal counting answers the question 'which one?', e.g. 4th house. Note that there is no 4-ness about it. Ordinal numbers rarely carry the word-endings, e.g. 4*th*, but must be clearly distinguished from cardinal numbers. (See Cardinal counting)

Place value refers to the way of writing numbers beyond those for which single numerals are available. The conventional base is 10, but smaller bases can be employed.

Quadriceps – The muscles at the front of the thigh

Quasi-transitive verbs are those which can, but do not always, carry grammatical objects, e.g. 'drink', or 'drink some water'; 'washed' or 'washed that car'. They are a convenient introduction to transitive verbs. (See Intransitive and Transitive verbs)

Seriation is arranging in order of size with equal steps between each item, as a normal staircase, or the marks on a ruler. It is a specific form of grading. (See Grading)

Transitive verbs carry grammatical objects, e.g. 'Do you like the flowers?', not 'Do you like?'. (See Transitive and Quasi-transitive verbs)

References

BERNSTEIN, L. 1976: *The Unanswered Question*. Cambridge, Mass.: Harvard University Press.

BUNZL, M. 1972: *Vocabulary Pack* (100 line drawings) London.: Invalid Children's Aid Association.

BUNZL, M. 1972: *Story Pack* (line drawings for 10 simple stories). London: Invalid Children's Aid Association.

BURROUGHS, G. E. R. 1957 Reprinted 1963: *A Study of the Vocabulary of Young Children*. University of Birmingham Institute of Education, Educational Monographs No. 1. Edinburgh and London: Oliver & Boyd.

CHURCHILL, E.M. 1962: *Counting and Measuring. An approach to Number Education in the Infant School*. London: Routledge & Kegan Paul.

CONN, P. Reprinted 1973: *Language Therapy I: Remedial Syntax*. London: Invalid Children's Aid Association.

COOPER, J., MOODLEY, M. and REYNELL, J. 1978: *Helping Language Development*. London: Edward Arnold.

CRYSTAL, D. 1979: *Working with LARSP*. Studies in Language Disability and Remediation 1A. London: Edward Arnold.

CRYSTAL, D., FLETCHER, P. and GARMAN, M. 1976: *The Grammatical Analysis of Language Disability: a Procedure for Assessment and Remediation*. Studies in Language Disability and Remediation I. London: Edward Arnold.

CUISENAIRE, Numbers in Colour (Box of rods) Reading, Berks.

DONLAN, C. and GILLIES, M. 1981. *Language Through Reading, Two*. London: Invalid Children's Aid Association.

EDWARDS, R. P. A. and GIBBON, V. 1964: *Words your Children use*. London: Burke Publishing Co. Ltd.

FERNALD, G. 1943: *Remedial Techniques in the Basic Subjects*. New York and London: McGraw-Hill Book Co. Inc.

GILLIES, M. and HUTT, E. 1985: *Language Through Reading, One*. London: Invalid Children's Aid Association.

GORDON, N. and McKINLAY, I., 1980 *Helping Clumsy Children*. London: Churchill Livingstone.

GORMAN, P. 1983: *The Paget-Gorman Sign System for Language Development*. (Paget-Gorman Society Newsletter, September 1983)

GRIFFITHS, P. 1972: *Developmental Aphasia: an Introduction*. London: Invalid Children's Aid Association.

GRIFFITHS, C. P. S. 1969: A follow-up study of children with disorders of speech. *British Journal of Disorders of Communication* IV, 46–56

HART, N. W. M., WALKER, R. F. and GRAY, B. 1977: *The Language of Children. A Key to Literacy*. London: Addison-Wesley Publishing co. Inc.

HASTIE, J. and ANDERSON, R. 1974: *Margaret Morris Movement Basic Exercises* (5th edition).

HUTT, E. 1973: *Teaching Symbolic Communication Skills*. London: Invalid Children's Aid Association.

LEA, J., 1970 *Colour Pattern Scheme*. Oxted, Surrey: Moor House School.

MACKAY, D., THOMPSON, B. and SCHAUB, P. 1970: *Breakthrough to Literacy*. Schools' Council. London: Longman's.

MORRIS, M. 1971: *My Life in Movement*. London: Peter Owen.

PAGET, R., GORMAN, P. and PAGET, G. 1976 (6th edition): *The Paget–Gorman Sign System*. London: Association for Experiment in Deaf Education.

PALMER, M. 1980: Why structure? Unpublished talk, ICAA Symposium.

SENATOR, R. 1977: *Musicolour*. Copyright Musicolour Ltd.

TYACK, D. 1976: *Children's Production and Comprehension of Questions*. (unpublished monograph): San Francisco State University.

VANDERSPAR, E. 1985: *Dalcroze Handbook: Principles and Guidelines for Teaching Eurhythmics*.

WHITE, J.W. 1980: *A Prophet without Honour*. Glasgow: Margaret Morris Movement Therapy.

Language Through Reading, One, is available from:
Publications, Invalid Children's Aid Association, 126, Buckingham Palace Road, London, SW1W 9SB. So is the current information on the publication of:
Booklets – on drama, Musicolour, mathematics, religious education, spelling, etc.
Drawings – action pictures (100 line drawings)
Grammatical sequence
Language Through Reading, Three
Materials – for handwriting, number, spelling, etc.
Tests – for number and spelling.
Vocabulary lists.

Language Through Reading, Two is available from:
Learning Development Aids, Duke Street, Wisbech, Cambs, PE 2AE.

Index

adjectives 7, 14, 30, 48, 52
adverbs 7, 14, 30, 47
association 9, 10, 118, 119, 143
attention 9, 10, 31, 50, 91, 92, 96, 107, 109, 143
auditory skills 9, 10, 31, 72, 74, 92, 93, 95, 109, 110, 112, 115, 125

balance 95, 100, 101, 104
balancing (math.) 137-8
bases (math.) 134-5
Basic Greek positions 104-5
basic signs 28, 35
Bernstein, L. 109
Bliss-symbols 54
body-awareness 96, 106, 107
Breakthrough to Literacy 13
breathing 98, 99, 100, 102, 103
British Sign Language 27
Burroughs, G.E.R. 6, 17

Campkin, M. 111
capital letters 24
cardinal (math.) 127, 128, 130
clauses 11, 41, 48, 51
closed-class word 11, 27, 30, 36, 54, 60, 63, 67, 74, 78, 120
colour 7, 11, Ch. 2, 42, 45, 52, 54, 62, 88-9, 112, 113, 133
Colour Factor rods 111
Colour Pattern Scheme 13
communication 9, 11, 26, 28, 31f, 35, 36, 37, 87, 94
commutation 138
comparative 30, 77
comprehension 6, 39, 57, 59, 96, 143
computing 140
concept-formation 96, 119-20
conjunctions 4, 14, 30, 39, 47, 62
consonant blends 81
consonant digraphs 81
Cooper, J., Moodley, M., and Reynell, J. 10, 96, 142
coordination 10, 21, 32, 86, 102, 109, 144
core-vocabulary 6
counting 130
counting-on 139
Cuisenaire rods 111

curriculum 5, 6f, 11, 143

Dalcroze 117
Dawn House School 142
Derbyshire Language Programme 142
determiners 4, 14, 30, 39, 48, 52, 63
Developmental Sentence Scoring 47
drawing 9, 10, 51, 59, 61, 67, 86, 87
duple time 103, 110

Edwards, R.P.A., and Gibbon, V. 6, 17
elicitation of questions, 50
  of statements, 43
elision 77
ellipsis 42, 52
environment *See* Ch. 12
expression 87, 96, 144
expressive disorder 3, 33, 54

feely box 93
Fernald, G. 72
finger-tracing 23, 72f
flash-cards 14
folders 11, 13-14
formation of letters, 23ff

Garthwaite, P. 108
gender 36, 40
gesture 8, 10, 27, 39
goals 9, 26, 51
Gordon, N, and McKinley, I. 95
grading 125, 128, 135
grammar 2, 11, 13, 39, 42 ,121
Grammatical Sequence 61
Griffiths, P. 142

handwriting 8, 11, Ch.3, 61, 79, 131
Hart, N.W.M., Walker, R.F., and Gray, B. 6, 17, 66
Helping Clumsy Children 95
Helping Language Development 10, 96, 98, 142
human nouns 14, 43, 51
hundred square 132-3, 135, 140

ideographic 9, 42
imagination 19, 87, 88, 93